CONNECTED REALMS

UNDERSTANDING MULTIPLAYER VIDEO GAMES

server | PLAY NOW

HENRY HANLEY

Email Enquiries please send to: henryhanley@hotmail.co.uk

Please leave feedback on this book on whichever platform it was purchased on. This encourages and motivates me to continue producing books, improving where I can, based on the feedback from customer reviews.

I would like to thank you for reading this book and I hope you enjoy!

Chapter 1 - Multiplayer Gaming and its rise to Stardom

In the ever-evolving realm of gaming, the term "multiplayer game" sparks thoughts of exhilarating adventures that extend far beyond the individual experience. From embarking on online conquests that bridge continents to joining forces with friends in cooperative quests, multiplayer games have reshaped how we dive into virtual worlds and connect with fellow gamers.

At its core, a multiplayer game offers a digital playground where multiple players can interact, collaborate, or compete within the same virtual universe. These games break free from the confines of solitary gameplay, offering a platform for players to come together in real-time, sharing their triumphs, facing challenges, and uniting in a realm of camaraderie.

The world of multiplayer interaction spans a spectrum, catering to diverse player tastes:

Teamwork Takes Center Stage: In cooperative multiplayer games, players unite to tackle common goals. Whether a squad of adventurers conquering epic quests or survivors teaming up to overcome hurdles, cooperation reigns supreme. Titles like "Destiny 2" and "Overcooked" thrive on players harmoniously collaborating to achieve shared victories.

Unleash the Competitive Spirit: Competitive multiplayer games throw players into showdowns where the ultimate prize is victory. Whether in one-on-one duels or team-based showdowns, these games celebrate strategy, skill, and the adrenaline of competition. Notable examples include "Fortnite," "League of Legends," and "Rocket League."

Waves of Interaction: Asynchronous multiplayer introduces a unique twist. It lets players engage with each other without requiring simultaneous interaction. Think leaderboards, ghost races in racing games, or taking turns in strategic gameplay. Players contribute their moves at different times, shaping the shared experience through their actions.

Crafting a Social Fabric
Creating the social fabric within multiplayer gaming involves weaving a tapestry of connections that span continents, forging friendships that transcend screens, and igniting rivalries that add excitement to every match. It's about uniting players from diverse cultures, fostering camaraderie through shared adventures, and celebrating the competitive spirit that turns virtual arenas into global stages of interaction and engagement.

Beyond the mechanics lies a vibrant social realm within multiplayer games:

Bridging Continents: Multiplayer games transcend geographical barriers, forging bonds among players from diverse cultures. Gamers forge connections spanning continents, fuelled by shared interests that know no boundaries.

Friendships and Friendly Rivalries: Gaming often blossoms into lasting virtual friendships. Shared experiences lay the foundation for camaraderie that extends beyond the game. Alongside friendships, good-natured rivalries add a touch of excitement, motivating players to enhance their skills and engage in playful banter.

Elevating Competitions: Multiplayer's competitive nature has given birth to the phenomenon of esports. Players now showcase their talents on global stages, captivating audiences with their strategies and skills.

A Glimpse into the Future
The world of multiplayer gaming is ever-advancing. Evolving technology introduces new dimensions, like virtual reality (VR) and augmented reality (AR), promising to elevate multiplayer

experiences. These innovations immerse players in shared virtual realms, while cross-platform play shatters barriers, enabling players on different devices to interact seamlessly.

Multiplayer games redefine the gaming landscape by fostering connections that transcend screens. The ability to unite players in ways unimaginable before has given birth to collaborative quests, fierce battles, and enduring friendships. As technology continues its journey, multiplayer gaming will undoubtedly expand its horizons, offering immersive, interactive, and socially enriching experiences that captivate players worldwide.

A Brief History of Multiplayer Gaming

The early history of multiplayer gaming is marked by innovations that set the stage for the dynamic and interconnected gaming experiences we know today. Lets take a look into the origins of multiplayer gaming and how it has evolved over time, highlighting and showcasing the pivotal moments that have shaped its trajectory to the present day.

Arcade Era and Local Multiplayer

The roots of multiplayer gaming can be traced back to the arcade era of the 1970s and 1980s. During this time, arcade cabinets like Pong and Space Invaders allowed players to compete directly against each other, sharing the same physical space and screen. These local multiplayer experiences laid the groundwork for the social aspect of gaming, as players engaged in friendly competitions and cooperative play side by side.

Arcades offered not only addictive gameplay, amazing graphics when compared to home consoles of the day, but a social aspect as well. Random people waiting their turn to play, or if it was a 2 or more player arcade machine, people would approach the machine and ask to join you, or just insert money in instantly to get in on the action. This is like the online gaming lobbies we have today, were you play total strangers you have never met before, or with friends.

The social aspect of arcades was much more enriching back in the day than the online gaming lobbies we join today to play games, as people used to cheer you on when getting closer to a high score in the arcade, congratulate you on how far you got if you were the first player to ever get past a bit everyone else was stuck at or to pass on friendly tips and advice if you kept getting killed in the same way over and over again to save you some coin.

Home Consoles and Couch Co-op
With the advent of home gaming consoles, the concept of local multiplayer found its way into living rooms. Games like "Super Mario Bros." introduced couch co-op, enabling players to work together to navigate challenging levels and defeat enemies. This introduced a new dimension of teamwork and communication, as players strategised and coordinated their actions.

This also saved people a lot of money, as trips to the arcade became less frequent once popular arcade titles started to get ported over to consoles people had at home. Gone were the jingling noises of people walking past who had loads of change ready to put into the arcade machines, when you heard the jingling, you knew they were either going or returning from the arcade. Most people went with a pocketful of change and came back with nothing but awesome memories and a good days gaming.

Rise of LAN Parties
As technology progressed, LAN (Local Area Network) parties became a popular way for players to connect their computers and engage in multiplayer matches. Games like "Quake" and "Counter-Strike" fuelled the LAN party phenomenon, where players brought their PCs together for intense multiplayer battles. This marked the early stages of competitive gaming and showcased the potential of connected gameplay beyond traditional split-screen experiences.

LAN parties are amazing, in the early days of Halo, there was no online multiplayer and it was all LAN based or local play on a single original Xbox. Only 4 people could play on a single Xbox at a time, but if it was 2 versus 2 players, you could always know where they were located on the map due to being able to see their screen which made it less fun.

Linking up 4 Xboxes to a switch, plus four TV's and miles of LAN cables connecting each Xbox to the switch, made the floor like spaghetti junction and possibly a serious health and safety risk. However, playing 16 player on a LAN on the original Halo game was just so worth it, no matter how much mess was left behind when they left from drink cans, crisp packets and chocolate from the 16 guests you had invited round to your house to play.

Online Multiplayer and the Internet Revolution
The true transformation of multiplayer gaming came with the widespread adoption of the internet. As broadband internet became more accessible, online multiplayer took centre stage. Games like "Diablo" and "StarCraft" introduced players to a new era of global connectivity, where they could challenge opponents from different parts of the world. This marked the birth of a virtual playground where players could engage in battles, quests, and collaborations regardless of their physical location.

Massively Multiplayer Online Games (MMOs)
The late 1990s and early 2000s saw the emergence of MMOs, a genre that took multiplayer gaming to a grand scale. Games like "World of Warcraft" and "EverQuest" allowed thousands of players to inhabit expansive virtual worlds simultaneously. These games introduced dynamic player interactions, intricate economies, and the sense of shared exploration that defined the MMO experience.

The evolution of multiplayer gaming showcases how technological advancements and changing social dynamics have shaped the way players interact and connect. From the early days of local multiplayer in arcades to the global reach of online multiplayer and MMOs, the journey has been one of innovation and community building. This historical overview sets the stage for understanding the continued evolution of multiplayer gaming and its profound impact on the gaming industry and entertainment landscape.

Technological Advancements and Connectivity

The world of gaming has come a long way since the early days of Pong and Space Invaders. Today, gamers are immersed in complex virtual worlds, collaborating with friends and challenging rivals from around the globe. This transformation has been driven by a series of technological advancements and the evolution of connectivity, shaping the multiplayer gaming landscape in ways that were once unimaginable.

The Power of Hardware Evolution

One of the cornerstones of multiplayer gaming's evolution is the advancement of hardware capabilities. The journey from basic 2D graphics to intricate 3D environments has been made possible by powerful graphics processing units (GPUs) and central processing units (CPUs). These components have enabled game developers to create visually stunning worlds that are not only immersive but also responsive.

As the computing power of GPUs and CPUs surged, games started resembling lifelike simulations. Players could now traverse expansive landscapes, experience realistic physics, and engage in dynamic interactions with the environment. The realism brought by hardware evolution has been a catalyst for transforming multiplayer experiences into truly interactive and captivating adventures.

Beyond Local Play - The Rise of Internet Infrastructure

The rise of multiplayer gaming as we know it would not have been possible without the expansion of internet infrastructure.

The transition from dial-up connections to high-speed broadband opened the floodgates for seamless online interactions. Gamers no longer needed to be in the same room to enjoy multiplayer experiences; they could connect with others across continents, sharing virtual adventures in real-time.

Faster internet connections drastically reduced latency, the nemesis of any serious gamer. The dreaded lag, that infuriating delay between an action and its result, became less and less prevalent. This shift meant that players could now engage in lightning-fast reactions, creating a smoother and more immersive experience overall.

This increased connectivity could have contributed to the popularity of arcades declining, as players could play from their own bedrooms or living rooms, without having to step a foot outside the door. Players can still interact with each other on online platforms such as Xbox Live for instance and can communicate with others via text and voice chat.

Redefining Social Interaction - Online Platforms and Services
Technological advancements brought forth dedicated online platforms and services that transformed multiplayer gaming into a social phenomenon. Platforms like Xbox Live, PlayStation Network, and Steam provided players with centralized hubs for matchmaking, voice chat, and community interaction. Friends could be invited to join matches, achievements could be unlocked and compared, and in-game marketplaces allowed for personalized character customization.

This redefined social interaction not only enhanced the gaming experience but also paved the way for esports and competitive gaming to flourish. These platforms gave birth to a new breed of gamers who found their passion in not just playing games, but mastering them and showcasing their skills on a global stage.

Matching Minds and Skill Levels - The Magic of Matchmaking

The concept of matchmaking revolutionized the way players connect in multiplayer games. No longer were players limited to friends within arm's reach; algorithms analysed player skill levels, play styles, and preferences to create balanced matches. This innovation struck a delicate balance between competition and enjoyment, ensuring that players faced challenging opponents while still having fun.

Cross-platform play emerged as another triumph of technology, allowing players on different devices to join forces or pit their skills against each other. This interconnectivity blurred the lines between gaming platforms and enabled a more diverse and inclusive player community.

Virtual Reality and Augmented Reality - The Next Gaming Frontier

As if the advancements in multiplayer gaming weren't thrilling enough, the introduction of virtual reality (VR) and augmented reality (AR) has pushed the boundaries even further. VR immerses players in entirely digital worlds, while AR overlays digital elements onto the real world. Both technologies have the potential to revolutionize multiplayer interactions, enabling players to communicate, cooperate, and compete in ways that were once the stuff of science fiction.

The Future Unveiled

In the ever-evolving landscape of multiplayer gaming, technological advancements and connectivity have been the driving forces that have changed how we play and experience games. As technology continues to advance, we can only anticipate more immersive, interconnected, and dynamic multiplayer experiences that will redefine our understanding of gaming. Whether it's the thrill of competitive esports, the camaraderie of cooperative quests, or the excitement of exploring virtual realms, the future of multiplayer gaming is brighter than ever before.

Matchmaking and Online Services: Elevating the Multiplayer Gaming Experience

In the realm of modern gaming, the experience of multiplayer matches has transcended physical boundaries and transformed into a digital symphony of competition, camaraderie, and connection. Central to this transformation is the ingenious concept of matchmaking and the evolution of online services. This article delves into the intricacies of matchmaking and explores the role of online platforms in shaping the multiplayer gaming landscape.

The Birth of Matchmaking

Long gone are the days when multiplayer gaming meant huddling around a single screen with friends. The advent of online multiplayer marked the dawn of a new era, where players could engage with opponents and allies from across the world. However, this transition brought along challenges, one of which was finding suitable opponents of similar skill levels.

Enter matchmaking, the digital wizardry that pairs players together in a way that's not only competitive but also enjoyable. No longer was your multiplayer experience determined by geographical proximity; instead, algorithms examined factors like skill, play style, and preferences to create balanced matches. This innovation transformed multiplayer gaming, making every encounter a thrilling test of skill, strategy, and teamwork.

The Art and Science of Balance

The heart of matchmaking lies in its ability to strike a balance between competition and fairness. Algorithms work tirelessly behind the scenes, taking into account various metrics to ensure that players are neither overwhelmed by superior foes nor underwhelmed by less experienced adversaries. This balance ensures that each match is a nail-biting experience, where victory is attainable yet hard-fought, creating a sense of accomplishment regardless of the outcome.

Matchmaking's sophistication extends beyond individual matches. The concept of skill-based matchmaking (SBMM) ensures that players are consistently challenged and engaged. Over time, players are matched against opponents of similar skill, fostering a sense of progression and improvement. This mechanism keeps the multiplayer landscape dynamic and prevents the frustration of being constantly outmatched.

Online Platforms - The Glue that Binds

Beyond the brilliance of matchmaking, online platforms have elevated multiplayer gaming to new heights. Platforms like Xbox Live, PlayStation Network, and Steam have transformed from mere gateways to immersive social spaces where players interact, compete, and form communities. Friends can be invited to matches, achievements can be showcased and compared, and voice chat allows for real-time strategizing.

Moreover, these platforms have been instrumental in bringing esports to the forefront. Tournaments, leader boards, and competitive events have found a digital home, creating an ecosystem where gamers can transform their passion into a professional pursuit. The integration of these services has made multiplayer gaming not just a pastime, but a lifestyle and a career choice.

The Path Forward

As technology continues to evolve, so does the realm of matchmaking and online services. The advent of cross-platform play has blurred the lines between gaming platforms, enabling even more diverse player interactions. Furthermore, the rise of cloud gaming promises a future where the need for powerful hardware is diminished, making multiplayer gaming even more accessible to a wider audience.

Matchmaking and online services are the unsung heroes that have transformed multiplayer gaming into a dynamic, immersive and socially connected experience. The algorithms that pair players and the platforms that provide a virtual haven for interaction have forever changed the way we engage with games. As we venture into the future, the role of these mechanisms will only become more pronounced, enriching the multiplayer gaming landscape with unprecedented possibilities.

Cloud Gaming and Remote Play - Redefining the Boundaries of Gaming

The world of gaming is on the cusp of a monumental shift, thanks to the emergence of cloud gaming and remote play. These groundbreaking technologies have the potential to revolutionize the way we experience games, breaking down barriers and granting players unprecedented access to their favourite titles.

Unveiling Cloud Gaming
Cloud gaming, also known as game streaming, represents a seismic leap in how games are delivered and played. Traditional gaming requires hefty hardware to run graphically demanding titles, but cloud gaming turns this notion on its head. Instead of running games locally, cloud gaming harnesses the power of remote servers to handle the processing and rendering, while delivering the final output to players' devices in real-time.

The magic lies in the concept of streaming. Players initiate a game on their device, which connects to a powerful server farm running the game. The server handles all the heavy lifting, rendering the game and sending the video feed back to the player's device. This means that even low-end devices like smartphones, tablets, or budget laptops can potentially run graphically intensive games, as the processing is outsourced to the cloud.

Remote Play - Gaming on Your Terms
Remote play, a close sibling of cloud gaming, takes a different approach. Instead of streaming games from a remote server,

remote play allows players to access and control their own gaming hardware from a different location. Imagine being able to play games from your powerful gaming PC at home while you're on the go, using a lightweight laptop or even a smartphone.

The mechanics are simple yet profound. Players install software on their gaming PC that enables them to access and control it remotely. This means that you can tap into your high-end hardware from virtually anywhere, as long as you have a stable internet connection. Remote play not only liberates you from the confines of a single location but also ensures that you're always gaming on hardware optimized for performance.

Benefits Beyond Convenience

Both cloud gaming and remote play bring a slew of benefits beyond the convenience of playing anywhere, anytime. For cloud gaming, the hardware requirements for players are dramatically lowered. You no longer need to invest in a top-of-the-line PC or console to enjoy the latest titles; a decent internet connection and a compatible device are all you need.

Remote play, on the other hand, bridges the gap between hardware capabilities. It allows players to harness the power of their primary gaming machine regardless of where they are. This democratization of hardware resources ensures that players can enjoy top-notch performance even on devices that wouldn't typically support high-end gaming.

Challenges and the Road Ahead

While cloud gaming and remote play hold immense promise, they are not without challenges. Both technologies heavily rely on stable and robust internet connections. The quality of the gaming experience is contingent on minimal latency and consistent bandwidth. Additionally, concerns regarding data usage and potential subscription costs for cloud gaming services have also surfaced.

As the technology evolves, these challenges are likely to be addressed. Companies are investing in data centres and networking infrastructure to minimize latency and provide a smoother experience. The growing adoption of 5G technology also holds promise for reducing latency and enhancing the feasibility of cloud gaming and remote play.

Cloud gaming and remote play are poised to reshape the gaming landscape, making high-quality gaming experiences accessible to a wider audience. These technologies transcend the limitations of hardware, enabling players to explore their favourite titles without constraints. While challenges remain, the potential benefits are too compelling to ignore. As the industry continues to innovate and invest in these technologies, the day might not be far when players can truly game on their own terms, unrestricted by the limitations of location or hardware.

The Power of Real-Time Communication in Today's Gaming Landscape

In the digital age, gaming is no longer confined to solitary experiences. It has transformed into a realm of vibrant communities, collaborations, and competitions that span the globe. A significant catalyst behind this evolution is real-time communication, an intricate web of technology that connects players in unprecedented ways.

Origins and Evolution
The roots of real-time communication in gaming can be traced back to the early days of multiplayer experiences. Initially limited to text-based chats and rudimentary voice options, the concept took a giant leap with the advent of the internet and advanced gaming platforms. The inclusion of voice chat brought a tangible sense of presence, enabling players to communicate naturally and immerse themselves in the virtual worlds they inhabit.

From basic voice communication to sophisticated cross-platform chat systems, the journey of real-time communication mirrors the rapid advancements of modern technology. Today, gamers can interact seamlessly with friends, team members, or opponents across different devices and geographical locations, creating a virtual camaraderie that transcends the boundaries of the screen.

The Role of Real-Time Communication
Real-time communication is more than just a medium for conversation; it's a dynamic tool that shapes the gaming experience on multiple levels:

Strategic Collaboration: Multiplayer games demand coordination and strategy. Real-time communication empowers players to devise and adapt strategies on the fly, facilitating complex manoeuvrers and calculated teamwork. It transforms games from individual exploits into collaborative journeys where success hinges on effective communication.

Social Bonds: Gaming has evolved into a global culture, uniting players from diverse backgrounds. Real-time communication fosters connections that extend beyond the confines of the game. It turns online interactions into genuine relationships, enabling players to forge friendships, alliances, and rivalries that are as tangible as they are virtual.

Community Building: Platforms like Discord and in-game chats have revolutionized community engagement. Players gather around shared interests, forming communities that nurture discussions, events, and collaborations. These platforms have become digital sanctuaries where enthusiasts congregate to share experiences, insights, and a mutual passion for gaming.

Esports and Streaming: Real-time communication isn't confined to in-game conversations. It has breathed life into esports and streaming. Audiences engage with streamers in real-time chats, share the excitement of competitive matches, and contribute to the narrative unfolding on-screen. This integration transforms gaming into a spectator sport, fostering a sense of unity among viewers.

Navigating Challenges
Despite its transformative potential, real-time communication isn't without its challenges. Issues like toxicity, harassment, and abusive behaviour have emerged as significant concerns. Developers are working diligently to create safer spaces, implementing features that allow players to report and mute disruptive individuals. The deployment of AI-driven solutions to identify toxic behaviour showcases the industry's commitment to fostering positive experiences.

The Future of Interaction
As technology continues its relentless march forward, the future of real-time communication holds promises of even greater immersion and interactivity. The rise of virtual reality (VR) and augmented reality (AR) introduces the possibility of nonverbal communication through gestures, expressions, and movements. This opens the door to a realm of interactions that go beyond language, providing players with new ways to express themselves and connect with others.

Real-time communication stands as an unseen but indispensable pillar of modern gaming. It bridges distances, fosters friendships, and enhances the gameplay experience in profound ways. As the gaming industry continues to innovate, real-time communication will remain a cornerstone that propels gaming from being just an individual activity to a communal pursuit that transcends screens, consoles, and continents. It's a testament to the power of technology to unite, engage, and immerse players in a world that's as real as it is virtual.

Chapter 2 - Types of Multiplayer Modes

Welcome to the world of gaming where multiplayer game modes are as diverse as the colours of a rainbow! Imagine teaming up with your pals to conquer missions together, or facing off in thrilling competitions that put your skills to the test. Whether you're coordinating strategies with your squad, exploring unique roles in asymmetrical games, or immersing yourself in sprawling worlds that never sleep, there's a multiplayer mode for every adventure seeker.

Don't forget the magic of cross-platform play, where you can join forces with friends no matter what device they're using. This means even if someone does not have the same console as you, you can still enjoy all the same games being played together online, oblivious as to what device anyone is playing it on.

Teamwork Makes the Dream Work - Cooperative Multiplayer (Co-op)
Imagine a gaming world where you and your buddies team up to conquer challenges together. Cooperative multiplayer modes let you do just that. Whether it's battling villains, solving puzzles, or completing missions, co-op games emphasize working as a squad. You'll share victories, strategize with your pals, and experience the thrill of teamwork.

Some examples of excellent cooperative multiplayer games are:

Overcooked! 2: Get ready to don your chef's hat and work together with your friends to prepare and serve dishes in chaotic kitchens. Time management and coordination are key as you navigate various challenges, from cooking on a hot air balloon to whipping up meals in a haunted house.

A Way Out: This game requires you and a friend to work together as two prisoners planning their escape. Navigate puzzles, make split-second decisions, and experience a unique split-screen cooperative gameplay that keeps both players engaged in the action.

Portal 2: In this mind-bending puzzle game, players must work collaboratively to solve intricate puzzles using portals. With one player controlling blue portals and the other controlling orange ones, communication and coordination are essential for success.

Lovers in a Dangerous Spacetime: In this charming and frantic co-op game, players control a spaceship's different stations to pilot through colourful, space-themed levels. Teamwork is vital as you control engines, shields, and weapons to fend off enemies and rescue cute space creatures.

Destiny 2: Embark on a sci-fi adventure as a Guardian, teaming up with friends to battle alien enemies and complete epic missions. From exploring lush landscapes to tackling challenging raids, Destiny 2 emphasizes cooperative gameplay in a dynamic online world.

It Takes Two: This cooperative action-adventure game follows two characters who have been magically transformed into dolls. Players must work together to solve puzzles, overcome challenges, and navigate a whimsical world filled with creativity and surprises.

Don't Starve Together: Survival takes on a new twist as you and your friends work together to gather resources, build shelter, and stave off hunger in a harsh and quirky world filled with creatures and mysteries.

May the Best Player Win - Competitive Multiplayer
Are you up for a showdown? Competitive multiplayer modes put your skills to the test in head-to-head battles against other players. It's all about outsmarting, out shooting, and outplaying your opponents. From classic death-matches to flag capture

and territorial control, these modes celebrate your gaming prowess and your ability to outwit rivals.

Some examples of high octane and competitive multiplayer games are:

Call of Duty: Warzone: Dive into the intense world of battle royale, where you'll engage in fast-paced firefights against dozens of players in a fight for survival. Whether you're scavenging for weapons or executing tactical strategies, Warzone is all about outlasting and outwitting your rivals.

Counter-Strike: Global Offensive (CS:GO): Join the ranks of terrorists or counter-terrorists in this classic first-person shooter. Teams compete in objective-based matches, where precise aiming, quick reflexes, and strategic coordination are the keys to victory.

Rainbow Six Siege: Step into the shoes of elite operators and engage in tactical battles in destructible environments. Each match requires teamwork, communication, and strategic planning to outmanoeuvre opponents and secure objectives.

Rocket League: Combine soccer and rocket-powered cars in this unique sports game. Teams compete to score goals by manoeuvring cars across the field, showcasing both driving finesse and aerial acrobatics.

League of Legends: Join the realm of MOBAs, where two teams of champions battle across a variety of maps and objectives. Combining strategy and skill, players work together to destroy the enemy's nexus while defending their own.

Valorant: Blend tactical shooting and hero abilities in this team-based shooter. Players select agents with unique skills, engaging in high-stakes battles where coordination and mastering each agent's abilities are crucial.

Fortnite: Immerse yourself in the vibrant world of battle royale, where you'll scavenge, build structures, and engage in frenetic gun-play to outlast other players. The game's building mechanics add an extra layer of strategy to the mix.

Capture the Flag in Halo Infinite: Halo's iconic multiplayer mode offers players the thrill of capturing the enemy's flag while protecting their own. Quick thinking, teamwork, and precision shooting are essential to securing victories.

Power in Numbers - Team-based Multiplayer

Grab your team colours and get ready to join forces! Team-based multiplayer modes split players into groups that face off against each other. Think of it as a virtual sports match where coordination, strategy, and communication lead your team to victory. Whether it's rescuing hostages or dominating control points, the camaraderie shines through.

Mixing It Up - Asymmetrical Multiplayer

Imagine a game where each player has a different role and goal. That's asymmetrical multiplayer for you! Some players might be fierce monsters while others are stealthy heroes. This mode throws exciting twists into the mix, creating a unique and unpredictable experience for everyone involved.

Every Gamer for Themselves - Free-for-All

Ready to show off your solo skills? Free-for-all modes turn every player into a lone wolf aiming to claim the top spot. Whether you're the last survivor standing or the player with the highest score, it's a test of your individual prowess in a chaotic, no-holds-barred environment.

Some iconic examples of games where lone wolves can shine by showing off their skills are:

PlayerUnknown's Battlegrounds (PUBG): Enter a battle royale arena where it's every player for themselves. Parachute onto a vast island, scavenge for weapons and gear, and strategically outplay opponents to secure the title of the last survivor standing.

Apex Legends: Dive into the fast-paced world of this battle royale game, where you choose from a variety of "Legends" with unique abilities. Whether you're forming temporary alliances or going solo, it's all about being the last legend standing.

Super Smash Bros. Ultimate: Gather your favourite gaming characters and engage in chaotic battles where the goal is to knock opponents off the stage. Free-for-all fights are a frenzy of attacks, dodges, and smash moves in a bid to claim victory.

Fall Guys: Ultimate Knockout: Jump, dive, and stumble your way through obstacle courses and mini-games in this colorful party game. Compete against other players in a series of whimsical challenges, with the aim of being the last Fall Guy standing.

Hearthstone: Engage in strategic card battles as you build decks and compete against opponents online. Test your tactical thinking, adaptability, and deck-building skills in a free-for-all environment where only the strongest strategist prevails.

Geometry Wars: Retro Evolved: In this intense arcade-style shooter, players navigate a vibrant grid filled with enemies and power-ups. With no allies to rely on, it's a fast-paced battle to survive and achieve the highest score possible.

Agar.io: Dive into the world of cells and growth in this online multiplayer game. Start as a small cell and consume smaller ones to grow larger. Compete against other players to become the largest cell in the arena.

Bomberman: Blast your way through a maze, planting bombs to eliminate opponents while avoiding their explosive traps. The free-for-all chaos demands strategic placement and timely detonations to reign supreme.

Living Worlds to Explore - Persistent World Multiplayer
Step into a virtual realm that's alive 24/7! Persistent world multiplayer games create vast playgrounds where you can explore, trade, and make friends. These worlds continue evolving even when you're not playing, giving you a sense of immersion and community that spans beyond just gaming sessions.

Some digital world's that exist outside are own physical world, are available in the following games:

World of Warcraft: Get ready for an adventure in Azeroth, a fantasy realm packed with diverse landscapes, dungeons, and stories. Join hands with fellow gamers, create guilds, and dive into battles against monsters and rival factions in this MMORPG.

EVE Online: Explore a massive space sandbox where you pilot ships, trade goods, and dive into strategic battles. With player-driven economics and politics, EVE Online's universe is shaped by massive space skirmishes and alliances.

Elite Dangerous: Take command of your very own spaceship and cruise through an open-world galaxy in this space simulation game. Trade, fight, and explore your way through a realistic portrayal of the Milky Way.

No Man's Sky: Embark on an exploration-packed journey across procedurally generated planets, star systems, and galaxies. Craft, build bases, and connect with alien species in an ever-expanding universe.

Final Fantasy XIV: Immerse yourself in the enchanting realm of Eorzea in this MMORPG. Join forces with friends for quests, raids, and dungeon runs while uncovering a spellbinding narrative filled with magic, creatures, and excitement.

Black Desert Online: Plunge into a breathtaking world where you can explore sprawling landscapes, engage in battles, trade goods, and even shape your property. With a deep character creation system and a dynamic day-night cycle, this game's got it all.

Albion Online: Step into the medieval fantasy world of Albion, where players wield influence over the economy, build settlements, and clash in intense PvP battles. The economy and sandbox mechanics keep the realm dynamic and ever-evolving.

Star Wars: The Old Republic: Immerse yourself in the Star Wars universe in this MMORPG. Pick your side – Galactic Republic or Sith Empire – and plunge into story-driven quests, epic space battles, and lightsaber duels.

Bridges Across Platforms - Cross-platform Multiplayer
Picture playing with your pals, no matter which gaming device they use. Cross-platform multiplayer lets you connect with friends on different systems, breaking down barriers and making the gaming world more inclusive than ever before.

The following games make multiplayer fun accessible to more people than ever before, as they can be played together, no matter what the console or device:

Fortnite: Battle Royale sensation Fortnight lets players join forces, no matter if they're on a console, PC, or mobile device. Friends from various platforms can squad up, strategize, and compete in the same matches.

Minecraft: Build, explore, and create with friends regardless of whether they're playing on Xbox, PlayStation, Nintendo Switch, or PC. Minecraft's cross-platform compatibility allows everyone to collaborate on massive projects.

Rocket League: This high-octane soccer-with-cars game lets players compete and cooperate across different platforms. Whether you're on a console or PC, you can team up and face off in thrilling matches.

Call of Duty: Warzone: Join the epic battle royale action in Warzone and fight alongside friends playing on different platforms. Cross-play support ensures you can form squads without platform barriers.

Among Us: Work together (or sabotage) with friends regardless of whether they're on mobile devices, PCs, or consoles. Deduction and teamwork are key to uncovering the impostors among the crew.

Paladins: Jump into this fantasy shooter and choose your champion to engage in cross-platform battles. Whether you're on Switch, Xbox, PlayStation, or PC, you can face off in exciting matches.

Dauntless: Team up with friends on different platforms to hunt down monstrous creatures in this free-to-play action RPG. Cross-play ensures you can battle side by side, regardless of your device.

Realm Royale: Enter the realm of fantasy battle royale and team up across platforms to be the last team standing. Cross-play allows for cooperative gameplay no matter where you're playing.

Game Nights with Friends - Local Multiplayer
Round up your buddies, grab your controllers, and settle in for some good old local multiplayer fun. These modes let you play together in the same room, whether it's split-screen racing or couch co-op adventures.

Here are two games that are best played locally, offer lots of competitiveness and fun, and are also great for playing when having a party to keep guests entertained:

Super Smash Bros. Ultimate: Gather your pals and engage in chaotic battles as iconic Nintendo characters. The fast-paced action and variety of stages make it a party favorite.

Mario Kart 8 Deluxe: Get ready for thrilling races and hilarious battles on crazy tracks. Mario Kart's accessible gameplay ensures everyone can join in on the fun.

Time to Take Turns - Asynchronous Multiplayer
No need to be online at the same time! Asynchronous multiplayer lets you take turns, and your actions impact the game even when your friends aren't playing. It's like sending challenges and surprises across time zones, keeping the excitement going.

Some examples of these type of games are:

Words with Friends: A modern take on Scrabble, this game lets you challenge friends to word-building duels. Take turns creating words on a virtual board, and your opponent responds whenever they're ready.

Draw Something: This Pictionary-style game lets you take turns drawing a chosen word while your friend guesses what it is. It's a creative and fun way to play together, even when you're not online simultaneously.

Chess with Friends: Challenge friends to a game of chess and make your moves at your own pace. The game notifies you when it's your turn, allowing for leisurely strategic play.

Letterpress: A word game that combines strategy and vocabulary. You create words to capture tiles and gain points. The game proceeds as players take turns forming words.

Trivia Crack: Engage in trivia battles with friends on a variety of topics. Answer questions and challenge your opponent's knowledge, all at your own pace.

Ticket to Ride: This digital adaptation of the popular board game allows you to build train routes across a map. Players take turns to claim routes and complete objectives.

Disc Drivin' 2: A fun and quirky racing game where you take turns flicking your disc along tracks. It's a mix of strategy and skill, and you can play multiple matches asynchronously.

Hero Academy 2: Engage in tactical battles with teams of fantasy characters. Players take turns planning their moves and attacking in this asynchronous strategy game.

Warpips: A real-time strategy game where you deploy armies and lead them into battle. While battles unfold in real time, players can take their time devising strategies between encounters.

Boggle with Friends: Shake the virtual letter dice, find words, and compete with friends to earn points. Players can play at their own pace in this asynchronous word game.

With such a colourful array of multiplayer modes, gaming transforms into a canvas of shared experiences. Whether you're all about teamwork, friendly rivalry, or exploring virtual worlds with pals, there's a multiplayer mode tailor-made for your unique gaming style. So gather your crew and dive into the exciting world of multiplayer gaming!

Overview of cooperative, competitive, and hybrid modes

Cooperative, competitive, and hybrid modes define the diverse landscape of multiplayer gaming. In cooperative modes, players join forces to overcome challenges, fostering teamwork and camaraderie. Competitive modes pit players against each other, where strategic thinking and skill determine victory.

Hybrid modes blend the best of both worlds, requiring players to collaborate while embracing individual competition. Each mode offers unique benefits: cooperation enhances social bonds, competition sharpens skills, and hybrid experiences strike a balance between unity and rivalry.

These modes cater to different player preferences, creating vibrant and dynamic multiplayer experiences that celebrate teamwork, skill, and the joy of shared victories.

Cooperative Multiplayer Gaming

In the ever-evolving world of gaming, cooperative modes have emerged as a pillar of multiplayer experiences, transforming how players interact, collaborate, and conquer challenges. From battling hordes of monsters to solving intricate puzzles together as one, cooperative modes have gained immense popularity due to their unique benefits, strong appeal and the competitiveness they bring to the table.

The Essence of Cooperation

Cooperative modes, also known as co-op, involve players teaming up to achieve shared objectives. These objectives can range from completing story missions to surviving against waves of enemies. Unlike competitive modes, where players face off, co-op modes encourage camaraderie and mutual support. Whether you're playing with friends or strangers, co-op gaming thrives on effective communication, strategising, and leveraging each player's strengths.

Benefits that Bind

The allure of cooperative gaming lies in its numerous benefits that resonate with players of all skill levels:

Teamwork Triumphs: Cooperative modes foster teamwork, teaching players the value of collaboration and effective communication. Players learn to coordinate actions, share resources, and complement each other's abilities, enhancing their overall gaming experience.

Shared Victories: Successfully conquering challenges together creates a sense of shared accomplishment. The satisfaction of working as a team and celebrating victories amplifies the enjoyment of the game.

Inclusivity: Cooperative modes cater to players with varying skill levels. Novices can learn from more experienced players, while veterans find joy in mentoring others, creating a supportive environment for everyone.

Social Bonds: Co-op gaming strengthens social connections. Playing with friends or meeting new players fosters friendships and provides a platform for shared experiences, even across distances.

The Attractiveness of Co-op

The appeal of cooperative modes is rooted in the emotional and psychological rewards they offer:

Empowerment: Co-op gaming empowers players by allowing them to contribute to the team's success. Everyone plays a crucial role, boosting player confidence and fostering a sense of significance.

Engagement: The unpredictability of co-op scenarios keeps players engaged. Collaborative problem-solving and adapting to dynamic situations keep the experience fresh and exciting.

Immersion: Cooperative modes often feature immersive narratives that draw players into compelling worlds. Shared storylines and experiences forge deeper connections between players and the game.

Positive Competition: While not competitive in the traditional sense, co-op modes introduce friendly competition through achievements, high scores, and efficient completion of objectives.

Competitiveness in Co-op

Competitiveness isn't absent from cooperative modes; it's

subtly woven into the fabric of teamwork:

Speed and Efficiency: Players often strive to complete objectives faster or more efficiently than previous attempts. This sparks friendly competition within the team to excel and optimize gameplay.

Role Excellence: Cooperative games often have diverse roles, encouraging players to excel in their specific roles, be it support, offence, or defence, driving healthy competition to perform exceptionally.

Challenge Conquering: Overcoming tough challenges together creates an inherent competition against the game's difficulty. Players aim to surpass these hurdles, driving a cooperative competitive spirit.

In a gaming landscape that often celebrates individual victories, cooperative modes offer a refreshing change of pace. They embrace unity, encourage teamwork, and demonstrate that victory is sweeter when shared.

As more players seek collaborative experiences that celebrate synergy over rivalry, cooperative modes stand as a testament to the power of friendship, strategy, and the joy of conquering virtual worlds together.

Competitive Modes in Multiplayer Gaming

In the realm of multiplayer gaming, competitive modes have emerged as a cornerstone, inviting players to engage in thrilling battles of skill, strategy, and wits. From epic shoot-outs to intense strategy matches, competitive modes have captured the hearts of gamers worldwide, offering a dynamic blend of benefits, irresistible appeal, and a competitive edge that keeps players coming back for more.

The Essence of Competition

Competitive modes, often referred to as PvP (Player versus

Player), centre around head-to-head battles between players or teams. These modes challenge players to outsmart, outmanoeuvre, and outperform their opponents to achieve victory.

Unlike cooperative modes that emphasize collaboration, competitive modes thrive on individual excellence and strategic thinking.

Benefits of the Battle
The allure of competitive gaming lies in its multifaceted benefits that resonate across player preferences and experiences:

Skill Development: Competitive modes demand mastery of game mechanics, honing players' reflexes, decision-making, and strategic prowess. The relentless drive to improve skills transforms gaming into a rewarding learning experience.

Personal Achievement: Victories in competitive modes evoke a sense of personal achievement. The rush of adrenaline upon outplaying opponents translates into a deep sense of satisfaction and accomplishment.

Strategic Thinking: Competitive modes cultivate strategic thinking and adaptability. Players learn to predict opponents' moves, devise counter-strategies, and make quick decisions under pressure.

Dynamic Challenge: The evolving nature of competitive gaming ensures that no two matches are alike. The challenge lies in decoding opponents' tactics and adjusting strategies on the fly.

The Allure of Competition

The attractiveness of competitive modes is grounded in the emotional and psychological rewards they offer:

Adrenaline Surge: The exhilaration of facing off against human opponents triggers an adrenaline rush, heightening players' senses and creating an intense emotional experience.

Social Interaction: Competitive gaming fuels interactions between players, fostering rivalries, friendships, and communities that form around shared interests and mutual respect.

Meaningful Progression: Competitive modes often feature ranking systems that showcase players' skill levels. Climbing ranks and achieving higher skill tiers provide a tangible sense of progression and growth.

Narratives of Triumph: The stories of overcoming tough opponents or executing perfect strategies become narratives of personal triumph, enriching players' gaming experiences.

Competitiveness Within Competition

Competitive modes not only showcase player skill but also introduce layers of internal competition:

Leaderboards: Competitive games feature leaderboards that display the highest scores or rankings. Players aim to ascend the leaderboards, sparking a competitive drive to claim a top spot.

Counter-play Dynamics: Players strategize against specific tactics or opponents, creating a competitive environment where counters and mind games are paramount.

Tournament Play: Organized competitive tournaments offer players the chance to test their mettle on a grand stage, fostering a spirit of competition within a broader community.

The Unending Pursuit of Victory
In a world where real-life achievements are often hard-won, competitive modes provide a digital arena for players to chase

victories, demonstrate their expertise, and experience the triumph of overcoming challenges. Whether competing for glory, recognition, or personal growth, competitive modes offer an electrifying landscape where players prove their worth, establish connections, and carve their path to virtual victory.

Hybrid Multiplayer Gaming

In the ever-evolving landscape of multiplayer gaming, hybrid modes have emerged as a dynamic fusion of cooperation and competition, inviting players to engage in gameplay experiences that defy conventional boundaries.

With a harmonious blend of teamwork and rivalry, hybrid modes offer a unique journey that encapsulates the benefits of both cooperative and competitive gaming, drawing players in with their distinctive appeal and an inherent competitive edge.

The Synergy of Hybrid Gameplay

Hybrid modes, also known as mixed modes, weave together elements of both cooperative and competitive gameplay. In these modes, players collaborate to achieve common objectives while simultaneously competing with each other to achieve individual milestones. The result is an intricate dance that challenges players to strike a balance between supporting their team and striving for personal success.

Benefits That Merge

The allure of hybrid gaming lies in the multitude of benefits that cater to players seeking a multifaceted experience:

Adaptive Playstyle: Hybrid modes encourage players to adapt their strategies on the fly. Balancing cooperation and competition requires a keen understanding of the game's mechanics and the dynamics of the team.

Collaborative Rivalry: Players engage in both cooperative teamwork and individual competition, fostering camaraderie among team members while keeping a competitive spark alive.

Flexibility in Roles: Hybrid modes often feature diverse roles that players can embrace, allowing them to contribute strategically to the team's success while pursuing personal achievements.

Strategic Depth: The interplay of cooperation and competition adds layers of complexity to gameplay. Players must navigate tactical decisions that impact their team and individual performance.

The Alluring Fusion

The attractiveness of hybrid modes stems from their ability to offer players a holistic gaming experience that encompasses diverse emotions and outcomes:

Dynamic Engagement: The alternating between cooperative and competitive phases keeps players engaged. The unpredictability of hybrid scenarios creates an environment where every moment counts.

Strategic Alliances: Collaborative play leads to the formation of temporary alliances within the team, fostering bonds that transcend the game and create memorable interactions.

Surprises and Twists: The fluid nature of hybrid modes introduces unexpected twists, adding excitement as players anticipate the ebb and flow between teamwork and rivalry.

Competitiveness Within Collaboration

While hybrid modes emphasize teamwork, elements of competition are intricately woven into the fabric of these experiences:

Personal Achievements: Players still pursue individual achievements even as they cooperate with their team. This creates an atmosphere where players push their limits to excel.

Dual Objectives: The dual nature of hybrid modes encourages players to balance objectives that contribute to both team success and personal glory.

Score-Based Triumphs: Hybrid modes often reward players based on individual accomplishments, driving players to outperform their teammates and rivals.

Harmony in Action
Hybrid modes exemplify the concept of gaming as an experience that transcends traditional boundaries. They showcase the ability of multiplayer games to blur the lines between cooperation and competition, offering players a tapestry of emotions, interactions, and challenges.

As players immerse themselves in the fluid dynamics of hybrid modes, they uncover the true essence of gaming as a collaborative competition and a competitive collaboration, where every move shapes a harmonious yet fiercely competitive symphony.

How Split Screen Gaming has Changed Over the Years

Split-screen multiplayer gaming has undergone significant changes over the years, evolving alongside advancements in technology, game design, and player preferences. From its humble beginnings on early consoles to its modern implementations, split-screen multiplayer has seen transformations that have both expanded and redefined the experience.

Early Days and Necessity
In the early days of gaming, split-screen multiplayer was born out of necessity. Limited hardware capabilities and processing power made it challenging to render multiple viewpoints on a single screen. Early consoles like the Atari 2600 and Nintendo

Entertainment System featured split-screen multiplayer in games like "Pong" and "Super Mario Bros." While the visuals were basic, split-screen allowed friends to play together in the same physical space.

Golden Age of Consoles
The 1990s and early 2000s marked the golden age of split-screen multiplayer. Consoles like the Super Nintendo, Sega Genesis, Nintendo 64, and PlayStation 2 introduced iconic multiplayer titles like "Mario Kart," "GoldenEye 007," and "Super Smash Bros." These games not only embraced split-screen multiplayer but also offered diverse game modes that catered to both cooperative and competitive play.

Challenges of Screen Real Estate
As gaming transitioned to more powerful consoles and higher graphical fidelity, split-screen faced challenges. Shrinking the screen for each player often led to reduced visibility and immersion. Some games mitigated this by employing dynamic split-screen, where the screen adjusted based on player positions or actions. However, this could still result in a compromised experience for players.

Online Multiplayer and Solo Experiences
The rise of online multiplayer in the late 2000s and early 2010s began to shift the focus away from split-screen. Players could now connect with friends remotely, reducing the need for local multiplayer. Additionally, single-player experiences became more immersive and story-driven, diverting resources and attention from split-screen modes.

Modern Iterations and Innovations

Recent years have seen split-screen multiplayer make a comeback, driven by demand from players seeking social gaming experiences. Developers have embraced split-screen in various ways:

Dynamic Split-Screen: Games like "Halo" and "Borderlands" implemented dynamic split-screen that adjusts the screen space based on player locations and actions, enhancing visibility and reducing visual clutter.

Couch Co-op Revival: Indie games like "Overcooked," "A Way Out," and "Lovers in a Dangerous Spacetime" prioritize local cooperative play, rekindling the joy of playing together with friends.

Hybrid Approaches: Some games, like "Rocket League," allow players to choose between split-screen and online multiplayer, offering flexibility in how players engage with their friends.

Mobile Devices: Mobile gaming has embraced split-screen on devices with larger screens, facilitating local multiplayer experiences on smartphones and tablets.

The Future of Split-Screen

As gaming technology continues to advance, split-screen multiplayer is likely to adapt and evolve. Games on next-generation consoles may leverage higher processing power to deliver smoother split-screen experiences with improved graphics. Additionally, split-screen could become a unique selling point for games on platforms that emphasize social interaction and local multiplayer.

In essence, split-screen multiplayer has traversed a journey of challenges, adaptations, and resurgence. While online multiplayer has transformed the gaming landscape, split-screen retains a special place in the hearts of players who value the tactile and social experiences it offers. As long as gamers seek shared moments of fun with friends, split-screen multiplayer will continue to find its place in the ever-changing world of gaming.

Chapter 3 - Networking Fundamentals

Network fundamentals are essential for seamless multiplayer gaming experiences. In a networked environment, players connect to servers or each other's devices to engage in real-time gameplay. Low latency, a stable connection, and sufficient bandwidth are crucial for minimizing lag and ensuring smooth interactions.

Reliable networking protocols enable data exchange, while security measures protect player privacy and prevent cheating. Whether playing cooperatively, competing head-to-head, or engaging in hybrid modes, understanding network fundamentals ensures that multiplayer gaming is immersive, responsive, and free from disruptions, enhancing the enjoyment of virtual worlds shared with friends and rivals alike.

Basics of network architecture in games

In the ever-evolving landscape of gaming, network architecture stands as the backbone of seamless multiplayer experiences. Behind the captivating graphics and immersive gameplay lies a complex web of technologies and protocols that enable players to connect, interact, and compete in real-time. From peer-to-peer connections to dedicated servers, understanding the basics of network architecture is essential for both players and developers, as it shapes the very foundation of modern multiplayer gaming.

Understanding Network Architecture
Network architecture in games refers to the underlying structure that facilitates communication between players and game servers. It's the framework that ensures data flows smoothly, minimizes lag, and creates an environment where players can engage in multiplayer activities without disruptions.

Client-Server Model
The client-server model is a cornerstone of network

architecture in gaming. In this setup, players' devices (clients) communicate with central game servers. Players send inputs to the server, which processes the data and sends updates back to all connected clients. This model centralizes game logic, ensuring consistency across all players and preventing cheating.

Peer-to-Peer Connections
In peer-to-peer connections, players' devices communicate directly with each other, bypassing a central server. While this can reduce latency, it also poses challenges like synchronization issues and potential security vulnerabilities. Peer-to-peer is commonly used in games with smaller player counts or in scenarios where a central server isn't necessary.

Latency and Bandwidth
Low latency (delay between sending and receiving data) and sufficient bandwidth (data transfer capacity) are crucial for smooth multiplayer experiences. High latency leads to lag, disrupting real-time interactions, while insufficient bandwidth can result in slow updates and degraded graphics.

Networking Protocols
Protocols like TCP (Transmission Control Protocol) and UDP (User Datagram Protocol) determine how data is transmitted between devices. TCP ensures reliable data transfer but may introduce latency, while UDP offers faster transmission but lacks error checking. Game developers often use a combination of both, prioritizing speed for gameplay-related data and reliability for critical information.

Load Balancing and Scaling
As player populations fluctuate, maintaining server performance is paramount. Load balancing distributes player connections across multiple servers to prevent overload. Scalability allows game servers to expand or contract based on demand, ensuring a consistent experience for players.

Security Measures

Network security is vital to prevent cheating, hacking, and unauthorized access. Encryption safeguards player data and prevents tampering, while measures like anti-cheat software detect and prevent unfair advantages. Secure connections are also essential for protecting players' personal information.

The Cloud and Beyond

Cloud computing has transformed network architecture by offering scalable, cost-effective solutions. Cloud-based servers reduce the burden on game developers, enabling them to focus on gameplay mechanics rather than server management. Additionally, cloud servers provide global accessibility and lower latency for players across different regions.

Network architecture is the invisible force that enables multiplayer gaming to flourish. It determines the quality of interactions, the speed of updates, and the overall gaming experience. From the client-server model to peer-to-peer connections, low latency to security measures, understanding these fundamental aspects is essential for both players and developers.

As technology advances, network architecture will continue to shape the future of gaming, delivering ever more immersive and seamless multiplayer experiences that bring players together across the virtual realm.

The Friendly Battle Between Client-Server and Peer-to-Peer Models

Ever wondered how multiplayer games let you play with friends or rivals from around the world? It's all thanks to network architecture, and there are two main ways games connect players: the client-server model and peer-to-peer setup. Let's dive into these options, break them down, and see what makes each one a great choice for different types of games.

Client-Server Model

Imagine the game server as the "boss" that makes sure everyone follows the rules. In this setup, your device (the client) chats with this big boss, and the boss controls the game's important stuff, like who's winning and what's happening. This helps keep things fair and stops cheaters. Plus, it makes sure everyone sees the same game, so no one has an advantage. It's like having a referee to keep the game exciting!

The benefits of the Client-Server Model are:

Fair Play: Cheaters, beware! The server keeps everyone honest and prevents any sneaky business from spoiling anyone's gaming fun. When it comes to the server, rules are not meant to be broken.

Same Game for All: Everyone gets the same updates from the boss, so the game is consistent for everyone. This means it creates a level playing field with no one having an advantage over another player from the get go.

Safety First: Your personal info is safe with the boss and unauthorized folks can't mess with your game.

Here are some downsides of the Client-Server Model:

Wait, Lag?: Sometimes, talking to the boss can take a bit of time to ask it something and get a response back, causing a tiny delay called "lag."

Money Matters: Setting up and maintaining the boss server costs money, especially for big games which has thousands or millions of players online at the same time.

Oops, Server Issues: If the boss server has problems, it can affect everyone's game. This means if the server goes down for instance, everyone will be affected. Normally people connect to servers in their own region or country. So if there was a single server for a game in the United Kingdom and it went down, but the United States had their own server for the game, only people connecting to the United Kingdom server would be affected.

Peer-to-Peer Model

Now, imagine a game where everyone talks directly to each other, like friends chatting in a group. This is what happens in the peer-to-peer setup. It's great for small games or when speedy chatting is important. Just remember, it's like hanging out with friends—you need everyone to agree and play nice.

Benefits of the Peer-to-Peer Model are:

Speedy Talk: Since everyone talks directly, there's less waiting and less lag. This will usually result in a more responsive experience, like when shooting at someone in a game, the bullets will hit and register on the enemy player when expected.

Sharing the Load: Everyone helps out, so no big boss server is needed, saving money. Data Packets are shared between users very quickly and the role isn't relying on one person doing this job.

Simple Stuff: The setup is easier to use and works well for smaller games. Most games using this model require you set-up a lobby within the game and then people search or find you in the games lobby or via IP address and join your game through an easy to use interface in the game menu.

Downsides of the Peer-to-Peer Model are:

Sync Struggles: Keeping everyone on the same page can be tough, leading to strange things happening in the game. Sometimes people can shoot a moving person in a first person shooter multiplayer game and they should be destroyed at a certain point, however they can run on a few more steps, then the game pulls them back to the point they should have been destroyed and registers as a point to the person playing. This can cause some widespread confusion when happening to multiple players in the game and seeing this taking place.

Tricky Business: Without a big boss, players could cheat or mess up the game. Some gamers may have mods installed on their game that a server would normally detect and not allow in the game to promote fair play between players.

Hit-or-Miss: The quality of connections between players varies, leading to some ups and downs. Some players will have broadband, some will have fibre and so forth. This means some players will have a better experience than other depending on the speed of their connections.

Choosing the Best Fit
Game developers pick between these models based on what kind of game they're making and what players want. Sometimes, they mix things up to get the best of both worlds! So, whether it's a boss-controlled game or a friends' chat, both models have their own magic that brings gamers together in fun and exciting ways.

Latency, bandwidth, and player experience

In the heart-pounding realm of online multiplayer gaming, every millisecond could mean the difference between a triumphant victory and a bitter defeat. As you embark on your virtual quests, two silent heroes work tirelessly behind the scenes: latency and bandwidth. These unsung champions of the gaming world wield immense power, shaping your gameplay experience in profound ways.

Unlocking the Secrets of Latency
Latency, or "ping," as gamers affectionately call it, is that mysterious delay between your controller inputs and the game server's response. Measured in milliseconds, latency's impact on your gaming experience is colossal.

Rapid Reflexes: Picture this – you're in a heart-pounding first-person shooter showdown. With low latency, your reactions are lightning-quick. You fire off shots and dodge enemy attacks with ease.

Precise Aim: A low-latency connection ensures that your every shot registers accurately. No more frustrating moments where you swear you hit the target, only to watch your opponent dance away unscathed.

Silky Smooth Gameplay: Low latency gifts you a seamless gaming experience. Your character moves and acts on-screen exactly as you command, with no noticeable lag. It's gaming nirvana.

Deciphering the Bandwidth Enigma

Bandwidth, measured in megabits per second (Mbps), is like the pipeline carrying all the gaming data between you and the server. Think of it as the width of that pipeline – the wider, the better.

Data Speedways: Bandwidth is the engine powering your gaming data. It ensures your game events, player positions, and even voice chat zip back and forth effortlessly.

Voice Chat Bliss: For those who love strategising with their squad or streaming their epic adventures, ample bandwidth means crystal-clear voice chat and buttery-smooth streaming.

How Does This Affect Your Gaming Adventure?

Battlefield Frustration: High latency can quickly turn your gaming experience into a whirlwind of frustration. Your actions seem to take ages to materialize, and in some cases, you might find yourself abruptly disconnected, leaving you feeling defeated.

Unlevel Playing Field: Lag imbalances can lead to cries of "unfair advantage." Players with lower latency tend to dominate, leaving those with high latency feeling like they're fighting an uphill battle.

Lag Compensation Drama: Game developers often employ lag compensation systems to level the playing field. While they aim to bridge the gap, they can sometimes introduce unpredictability into your gameplay.

Voice Chat Woes: Limited bandwidth can turn voice chats into a nightmare, as your squad's plans get muffled in a sea of choppy communication. In team-based games, that's not just frustrating; it's disastrous.

Data Dilemmas: Data caps imposed by your internet service provider can become the bane of your gaming existence. Excessive bandwidth usage from gaming, streaming, or those massive game updates might hit you where it hurts – your wallet.

Dominating the Gaming Realm
In the world of online multiplayer gaming, where epic victories and crushing defeats hang in the balance, latency and bandwidth emerge as the unsung heroes of your gaming saga. To embark on a truly victorious adventure, equip yourself with a low-latency, high-bandwidth internet connection and keep an eagle eye on that ping. With these tech-savvy allies by your side, you'll conquer virtual worlds and claim your place among the gaming elite.

Tips for reducing lag in games

In the realm of gaming, lag is the enemy. It's that infuriating delay that can make the difference between triumph and defeat. Whether you're on a console or PC, reducing lag is crucial for a smoother and more enjoyable gaming adventure. Here are some practical tips to help you achieve just that:

Streamline Background Services

On your PC, think of your game as the star of the show. Open the Task Manager and shut down any background processes or applications that are guzzling up precious system resources and bandwidth. Netflix, we're looking at you! Console gamers, don't fret. Make sure no unwanted background apps are running. Most consoles allow you to suspend or close these apps right from their menus.

Halt Downloads and Updates

Your excitement over downloading the latest games or updates might come back to haunt you if it hogs your bandwidth. To ensure an uninterrupted gaming experience, pause or schedule these downloads during your off-hours.

Xbox users can hit "Pause All" in "My games & apps," while PlayStation fans can halt downloads from the notifications menu. PC gamers, manage your downloads in your game launcher (like Steam or Epic Games Store).

Harness the Power of Ethernet

If you're serious about reducing lag, a wired Ethernet connection is your secret weapon. It's more stable and typically provides lower latency compared to Wi-Fi. Plug your console or PC directly into your router with an Ethernet cable for a rock-solid connection.

Tinker with Router Settings

Dive into your router's settings and check if Quality of Service (QoS) is activated. QoS prioritizes gaming traffic, ensuring that your gameplay gets the lion's share of bandwidth.

Don't forget to enable UPnP (Universal Plug and Play) to make sure your gaming device has the necessary port forwarding for online gaming.

Keep That Firmware Updated

Your router deserves some TLC too. Regularly update its firmware to ensure optimal performance and take advantage of bug fixes and enhancements.

Try a Gaming VPN

Sometimes, a gaming VPN can work wonders by optimizing your connection path. But keep in mind, it's not a one-size-fits-all solution and effectiveness may vary.

In-Game Optimization

Make friends with your game's settings menu. Lower graphics settings to ease the load on your GPU and CPU, resulting in improved performance and reduced lag.

Look for network settings in your game and fine-tune them to prioritize low latency and responsiveness.

Pick Your Servers Wisely

When venturing into the online gaming world, select servers with lower ping (latency) whenever possible. Playing on servers closer to your geographic location generally means smoother gameplay.

Give Your Router a Breather

Periodically restart your router and modem to shake off any cobwebs that might be hindering your gaming experience. A fresh start can work wonders.

Activate Gaming Mode (If Available)

Some modern routers feature a gaming mode or low-latency mode designed to optimize the network specifically for gaming. If your router boasts this feature, don't hesitate to enable it.

By applying these tips, you can level up your gaming experience and say goodbye to those frustrating lag spikes. Remember, while you can take control of your local network conditions, some elements of lag may be beyond your reach, such as server performance or the quality of the game's netcode. However, with these strategies in your arsenal, you'll be primed for gaming greatness.

Chapter 4 - Matchmaking and Lobbies

In the realm of multiplayer gaming, where virtual worlds come alive and friendships are forged in the heat of battle, there exists an invisible hand that guides every player's journey. Like a masterful conductor orchestrating a symphony, matchmaking is the unsung hero of this digital arena. It's the force that ensures every match is a thrilling adventure, where skill and strategy take centre stage.

Yet, its inner workings remain largely shrouded in mystery. In this exploration of the art and science of matchmaking, we peel back the curtain to reveal the secrets that shape our gaming experiences. Welcome to a world where fairness, fun, and fierce competition intersect, where matchmaking reigns supreme and where the future of gaming's most crucial element awaits.

The role of matchmaking in player pairing

In the vibrant world of multiplayer gaming, a seamless and enjoyable experience hinges on a delicate balance. Picture this: you're eagerly diving into an online match, heart racing, fingers poised on your controller or keyboard. You're about to enter a world where strategy, skill, and teamwork reign supreme. But what you might not realize is that a silent, complex force is at work behind the scenes, shaping your gaming experience—the art of matchmaking.

Understanding Matchmaking
Matchmaking is the digital cupid of multiplayer gaming, tasked with pairing players together for the ultimate showdown. Whether you're into team-based shooters, battle royales, or cooperative adventures, matchmaking is the linchpin that ensures you face opponents or allies who are on a similar skill level.

How Does Matchmaking Work?

At its core, matchmaking employs a two-fold approach:

Player Skill Rating: Every player in a game typically has a hidden skill rating or matchmaking rating (MMR). This rating reflects your skill level, based on factors such as your win-loss ratio, individual performance metrics, and in-game achievements. Think of it as a digital representation of your gaming prowess.

Balancing Teams: Matchmaking systems strive to create balanced teams where the overall skill level of each team is roughly equal. This means that if you're an intermediate player, you're more likely to be paired with teammates and opponents of a similar skill level.

The Impact of Matchmaking
So, what makes matchmaking such a crucial component of the gaming experience?

Fairness and Fun: Matchmaking ensures that you don't find yourself in a lopsided match, facing off against players who significantly outclass or underperform compared to you. This promotes fair competition and an enjoyable experience for everyone involved.

Skill Growth: It provides an avenue for players to grow and improve. Facing opponents of similar skill levels encourages healthy competition, making it easier to identify areas for improvement and refine your gameplay.

Reduced Frustration: Remember those games where you felt completely overwhelmed or bored because the competition was either too intense or too easy? Matchmaking strives to minimize those experiences, offering a more consistent challenge level.

Shorter Queue Times: Matchmaking ensures you spend more time gaming and less time waiting in a lobby for opponents. It optimizes the pairing process, so you can dive into the action faster.

Challenges in Matchmaking

While matchmaking is designed to provide a balanced and enjoyable gaming experience, it's not without its challenges:

Smurfing: Some players deliberately create new accounts (known as smurf accounts) to manipulate the matchmaking system and face lower-skilled opponents. This can disrupt the fairness of matches.

Long Queue Times: In some cases, especially at extreme skill levels, the matchmaking system may struggle to find suitable opponents quickly, leading to extended queue times.

Algorithm Adjustments: Developers often fine-tune matchmaking algorithms based on player feedback and data analysis, which can sometimes lead to unexpected shifts in the matchmaking experience.

The Future of Matchmaking

As gaming technology continues to advance, matchmaking is poised to become even more sophisticated. Machine learning and AI-driven matchmaking systems are on the horizon, promising even more precise player pairings based on a multitude of factors, including play style and strategies.

In the world of multiplayer gaming, matchmaking ensures the battles are fierce, the alliances are strong, and the experience is memorable. So the next time you embark on a gaming adventure, take a moment to appreciate the intricate dance of algorithms and data that brings players together in the digital arena. It's matchmaking that keeps the thrill alive and the competition fair.

What happens if there are not enough people of a similar skill-set online?

When a matchmaking system cannot find enough players

within a particular skill range to create a match, it faces a dilemma: Should it match players with slightly higher-skilled opponents or slightly lower-skilled opponents? The choice largely depends on the design philosophy of the game and its matchmaking algorithm.

Here's how it typically works:

Matchmaking Range Expansion: Many matchmaking systems are designed to prioritize finding a match quickly. If there are not enough players within your skill range, the system may expand its search parameters. This means it might pair you with opponents who are either slightly higher or lower in skill. This trade-off prioritizes shorter queue times and a faster gaming experience over perfect skill balance.

Skill Gap Tolerance: Matchmaking systems often have a tolerance level for skill gaps. For example, it might allow for matches where the skill difference is within a certain percentage of your MMR (Matchmaking Rating). This ensures that even when you face slightly higher-skilled opponents, the difference is not overwhelming.

Balancing Factors: To maintain fairness, the matchmaking system may take into account other factors when creating matches, such as party size (if you're playing with friends) or in-game achievements. These factors can help mitigate the impact of skill disparities.

Adjustments Over Time: Some matchmaking algorithms track your performance in these situations. If you consistently perform well against higher-skilled opponents, your MMR may increase, and the system will gradually pair you with tougher opponents in the future.

Bot Matches: In certain cases, if there are still not enough players available, the game might substitute human opponents with AI-controlled bots to maintain a reasonable queue time.

It's important to note that different games and platforms may implement matchmaking rules differently. Some prioritize skill balance above all else, even if it means longer queue times. Others prioritize quick matches but try to keep skill disparities within reasonable limits.

Ultimately, the goal of matchmaking is to strike a balance between providing a challenging experience and minimizing waiting times. While it may not always achieve perfection in skill balance, it aims to create enjoyable and competitive matches that keep players engaged and entertained.

Creating effective lobbies and waiting rooms

In the world of multiplayer gaming, the excitement of joining a match is electrifying. Yet, what happens when you're in the lobby, waiting for the game to begin? Game developers understand the importance of creating an enticing waiting experience, where players feel engaged and connected even before the action starts.

Let's delve into the strategies and design elements that game creators use to craft lobbies and waiting rooms that captivate players and transform the wait into an integral part of the gaming experience.

Intuitive Interface
A user-friendly interface ensures that players can effortlessly navigate the lobby. It should be designed for easy access to crucial information and seamless interactions with other players.

Matchmaking Mastery
The heart of a good lobby lies in effective matchmaking algorithms. These algorithms aim to pair players of similar skill levels, enhancing the overall quality of gameplay.

Progress Clarity
Visual cues like progress bars or countdown timers keep players informed about the wait duration. Knowing that their wait won't be indefinite maintains player engagement.

Interactive Features
Entertaining distractions, such as mini-games, quizzes, or challenges, make the wait enjoyable. Games within the game keep boredom at bay.

Personalization Options
Personalization features, including customizable avatars, emotes, and cosmetic items, allow players to express themselves and have fun while waiting.

Communication Tools
In-game chat or voice chat facilitates interaction among players in the lobby. It can be a valuable tool for coordinating strategies or simply for socializing.

Spectator Mode
Spectator mode lets players observe ongoing matches. It's an engaging way to learn from others or just to enjoy the game while they wait.

Ready-Up Mechanism
A "Ready" or "Start" button encourages players to indicate when they're prepared to join the game, preventing delays due to AFK players.

Dynamic Visuals
Engaging visuals, such as animated backgrounds or interactive elements, create an immersive waiting room that captures players' attention.

Information Hub
Provide details about the upcoming match, like the map, game mode, or the opponents' team composition. This enables players to strategize or prepare accordingly.

Musical Ambiance
Music and sound play a significant role in setting the tone of the lobby. A catchy soundtrack or ambient tunes heighten the atmosphere.

Progression Incentives
Reward players for their patience or for participating in lobby activities. In-game rewards like experience points, currency, or cosmetic items can be motivating.

Clear Notifications
Keep players informed about the lobby's status—whether it's searching for players, initiating the match, or addressing any issues. Transparency minimizes frustration.

Accessibility Features
Ensure that the lobby is accessible to all players, including those with disabilities. Features like text-to-speech or adjustable text sizes promote inclusivity.

Creating an inviting lobby isn't just about passing time; it's about setting the stage for an exciting gaming experience. Game developers recognize that a well-designed lobby can build anticipation, foster social connections, and keep players engaged, ensuring that the wait is an enjoyable part of the gaming journey.

Balancing skill levels and player preferences

In the realm of multiplayer gaming, a symphony of diverse player skills and preferences converges on virtual battlefields daily. Game developers, the conductors of this digital orchestra, face the intricate challenge of harmonizing skill levels while catering to the unique preferences of their player base. But how do they strike that delicate balance, ensuring competitive matches that are also tailored to individual tastes?

Balancing Skill Levels: The Science Behind Fair Play

Creating balanced matches where skill disparities are minimized is a science in itself.

Game developers employ a variety of methods and algorithms to achieve this equilibrium:

Matchmaking Ratings (MMR): At the heart of many games' matchmaking systems is the MMR. It's a hidden rating that quantifies a player's skill level based on past performance. The MMR is used to match players with others of similar proficiency.

Elo System: Some games use the Elo system, a mathematical model pioneered in chess, to calculate player ratings and determine the likelihood of victory against opponents. The difference in Elo ratings dictates the potential outcome of a match.

Ranking Tiers: Many games feature ranking tiers or divisions, such as Bronze, Silver, Gold, etc. Players are grouped within their respective tiers, ensuring that those with similar skills face off.

Skill Gap Tolerance: Matchmaking systems often allow a small skill gap to keep queue times reasonable. They find a balance between skill balance and player wait times.

Party Size Consideration: When players team up with friends, developers factor in the combined skill level of the group to create balanced matches.

Handling Player Preferences - Crafting the Art of Choice
While balancing skill levels forms the foundation of a satisfying multiplayer experience, catering to player preferences adds depth and personalization. Game developers pay keen attention to several aspects:

Map and Mode Selection: Allowing players to choose specific maps or game modes helps align the gaming experience with their preferences. Some games use voting systems, while others offer rotating playlists.

Customization Options: Cosmetic customization, such as skins, emotes, and character appearances, lets players express their individuality. These preferences often lead to micro-transactions that sustain the game's development.

Role-Based Matchmaking: In team-based games, systems that assign players roles or positions based on their preferences ensure a well-rounded team composition and enhance player satisfaction.

Gameplay Features: Game developers frequently update their titles with new features and mechanics based on player feedback and emerging trends, ensuring the game evolves in line with player preferences.

In-Game Events: Limited-time events, challenges, and seasonal content cater to players seeking variety in their gaming experience. These events often tap into specific themes or themes to match player interests.

Communication Tools: Robust in-game communication tools, like voice chat, text chat, or ping systems, facilitate teamwork and social interaction, catering to players who value collaboration.

While there may not be a one-size-fits-all formula for balancing skill levels and player preferences, game developers constantly refine their approaches to strike the right chord. It's a continuous journey of data analysis, player feedback, and adaptation, all aimed at creating a gaming experience that is both challenging and enjoyable, a true symphony of skill and personal taste.

Game Servers and Infrastructure

Game servers and infrastructure are the backbone of

multiplayer gaming, serving as the digital arenas where players come together for matches and lobbies. Let's explore how they work in the context of lobbies and matchmaking.

Game Servers - The Hosts of Virtual Worlds

Game servers are specialized computers or clusters of computers responsible for hosting multiplayer matches. Each game session, whether it's a deathmatch in a first-person shooter or a battle royale showdown, typically runs on a dedicated game server. Here's how they function:

Match Hosting: When a match begins, the game server takes charge of managing the game world. It hosts the map, game rules, physics, and all the players' interactions within that session.

Player Interaction: Players send their actions (like movement, shooting, or using abilities) to the server. The server processes these actions and calculates the game state, ensuring that every player's actions are synchronized in real-time.

Data Transfer: To maintain synchronization, game servers send frequent updates to all connected players. These updates contain information about the game's current state, including player positions, scores, and events (like kills or objectives achieved).

Lag Compensation: Game servers often employ lag compensation techniques to ensure that players' actions are registered fairly. For instance, a player with a high ping may see a slightly different game state, but the server reconciles this to ensure fairness.

Security: Game servers also play a vital role in security by preventing cheating and unauthorized access. They validate player actions to ensure they conform to the game's rules.

Matchmaking and Lobbies - The Gateway to Gaming

Matchmaking and lobbies are key components that facilitate players' entry into multiplayer matches.

Here's how they work:

Matchmaking Algorithms: Matchmaking starts with algorithms that assess player skill levels based on various factors, such as performance history and MMR (Matchmaking Rating). These algorithms aim to create balanced matches by pairing players with similar skill levels.

Lobby Creation: Once a match is found, a lobby is created. A lobby serves as a virtual waiting room where players can gather before the match begins. Here, players can chat, customize load-outs, and prepare for the upcoming game.

Player Preferences: Matchmaking systems often consider player preferences when forming lobbies. These preferences may include preferred game modes, maps, or the option to play with friends. This ensures that players are matched in games they want to play.

Ready-Up Mechanism: To prevent players from going AFK (Away From Keyboard) and delaying matches, lobbies often include a ready-up mechanism. Players indicate their readiness, and once all players are ready, the match begins.

Dedicated Servers: In some cases, lobbies transition to dedicated game servers when a match starts. This ensures that the actual gameplay occurs on reliable, high-performance servers.

Post-Match Actions: After a match, players often return to the lobby, where they can view match statistics, chat with other players, and decide whether to continue playing together.

Server Selection: Some games allow players to choose their server regions, allowing them to play with friends or in regions with better latency.

Game servers and infrastructure are the invisible architects of the multiplayer gaming experience, ensuring that players can seamlessly connect, compete and socialize in virtual worlds. The intricate coordination between matchmaking, lobbies and dedicated game servers makes multiplayer gaming a dynamic and immersive adventure for players worldwide.

Chapter 5 - Building and maintaining game servers

In the captivating world of multiplayer gaming, where friends and foes unite in virtual arenas, there's an unsung hero working tirelessly behind the scenes—the game server. For those with a passion for gaming and a penchant for technology, building your own game server can be an exciting endeavour. Let's delve into the steps and considerations involved in creating your very own gaming haven.

Step 1: Define Your Game
Before you dive into the world of server construction, you need to decide which game you want to host. Whether it's a popular title or a custom game you're developing, understanding the game's requirements is crucial. Consider factors like the number of players it supports, the game engine it uses, and any specific networking needs.

Step 2: Hardware Selection
The heart of your game server lies in the hardware you choose. Your server hardware should align with the game's demands and the number of players you anticipate.

Here are some key hardware components to consider:

CPU: Opt for a robust CPU with multiple cores to handle the game's calculations efficiently.

RAM: Sufficient RAM is essential for running the game and managing player connections.
Storage: Use fast SSDs for quicker loading times and data retrieval.

Network Interface Card (NIC): Invest in a reliable NIC for stable network connections.
Cooling: Ensure your server has adequate cooling to prevent overheating during long gaming sessions.

Step 3: Choose Your Operating System
Select an operating system that's compatible with your game and offers the required server software support. Popular choices include Windows, Linux (e.g., Ubuntu or CentOS), and FreeBSD.

Step 4: Install Server Software
Depending on your game, you'll need to install the appropriate server software. Game developers often provide dedicated server software packages, which you can download and configure. Some games even have modding communities that create custom server software.

Step 5: Networking Configuration
Proper networking is essential to ensure players can connect to your server. You'll need to configure port forwarding on your router to direct incoming traffic to your server's IP address. Assign your server a static IP to prevent IP changes that can disrupt connections.

Step 6: Security Measures
Gaming servers can attract unwanted attention, so implement security measures to protect your server and its players. Consider using firewalls, intrusion detection systems, and regular security updates to safeguard your setup.

Step 7: Server Management
Once your server is up and running, you'll need tools for effective management. There are server management panels and third-party software that provide an intuitive interface for server administration, player monitoring, and moderation.

Step 8: Player Community and Moderation
A successful game server is more than just hardware and software; it's a community. Engage with your players, set up forums or Discord servers for communication, and establish rules and moderation policies to ensure a friendly and enjoyable environment.

Step 9: Maintenance and Updates

Regularly maintain your server by applying game updates, patches, and security fixes. Keep an eye on server performance and make upgrades as necessary to accommodate growing player numbers.

Step 10: Scaling Up

If your server becomes popular and attracts a substantial player base, consider scaling up by investing in more powerful hardware or exploring server hosting services to handle the increased load.

Building your own game server is a rewarding journey that combines technical expertise with a passion for gaming. By carefully selecting hardware, mastering server software, and fostering a vibrant player community, you can create a gaming haven where players from around the world gather to engage in epic battles and unforgettable adventures.

Scalability, load balancing, and server locations

In the dynamic universe of multiplayer gaming, where millions of players from across the globe converge for epic battles, the invisible heroes working behind the scenes are scalability, load balancing, and strategic server locations. These elements ensure smooth and exhilarating multiplayer experiences. Let's dive into their crucial roles and how they shape the landscape of online gaming.

The Significance of Scalability

Imagine a massive multiplayer online game where thousands of players simultaneously explore a vast, open world. As more players join the fray, the demand on game servers surges. This is where scalability comes into play.

Scalability, in the context of multiplayer gaming, refers to a server's ability to handle an increasing number of players and maintain performance.

To achieve this, developers employ several strategies:

Server Clustering: This involves adding more servers to a cluster as player numbers grow. Each server shares the load, ensuring that the game world remains responsive and stable.

Dynamic Resource Allocation: Scalable games adjust server resources (CPU, RAM, bandwidth) in real-time based on demand. This ensures optimal performance without overloading individual servers.

Load Balancers: Load balancers distribute incoming player connections across multiple servers, preventing any single server from becoming overwhelmed.

Load Balancing - The Virtuoso Conductor

Load balancing is the conductor of the multiplayer orchestra, ensuring that every player's experience is harmonious. Its primary function is to distribute incoming player connections, traffic, and game data across available servers. Here's how it works:

Player Distribution: When a player logs in or initiates a game session, the load balancer directs them to the least busy server. This avoids server congestion and ensures low latency gameplay.

Fault Tolerance: Load balancers detect server failures and reroute traffic to healthy servers. This ensures that a server crash doesn't disrupt the gaming experience.

Scaling Support: As the number of players fluctuates, load balancers automatically adjust the distribution of players to maintain performance.

Strategic Server Locations - The Geographical

Chessboard

Imagine you're playing a multiplayer game with someone on the other side of the world. The speed at which your data travels between your device and the game server can significantly impact your gameplay. This is where strategic server locations come into play.

Game developers strategically position servers in various regions worldwide to reduce latency and ensure a fair and enjoyable experience for all players.

Here's how it affects your gameplay:

Low Latency: Servers located closer to players result in lower latency (ping). This means actions in the game, like shooting or moving, register more quickly, creating a more responsive and competitive environment.

Fair Play: Balanced server locations prevent players from one region having an undue advantage over others. Everyone competes on a level playing field.

Localization: Some games localize servers to provide a culturally relevant experience, including language support and events tailored to specific regions.

Scalability, load balancing, and strategic server locations are the strong support columns of multiplayer gaming. They work tirelessly to ensure that millions of players can come together from around the world, engage in epic battles, and forge unforgettable memories. The next time you join an online gaming session, remember that these invisible forces are the ones making it all possible.

Server-side mechanics and synchronization

In the realm of multiplayer gaming, where players from different corners of the globe unite for epic showdowns, there's a computer working overtime in the background to keep everything in sync - server-side mechanics and synchronization.

These essential components are the invisible conductors orchestrating the symphony of online gaming, ensuring every action is coordinated, synchronized and fair. Let's delve into their crucial roles and how they shape the multiplayer gaming experience.

The Role of Server-Side Mechanics

In the world of multiplayer gaming, there's a fundamental question: "Who's in charge?" The answer is the game server.

Here's how server-side mechanics come into play:

Centralized Control: In multiplayer games, all players connect to a central game server. This server acts as the authoritative source of truth, managing the game world and ensuring consistency.

Action Validation: When a player performs an action, such as firing a weapon or moving, the game client sends that action to the server. The server validates the action to prevent cheating or unfair advantages.

Real-Time Calculation: Server-side mechanics calculate the game's state in real-time. This includes player positions, damage calculations, and environmental interactions, all while keeping everything synchronized among players.

Anti-Cheat Measures: Server-side mechanics play a vital role in anti-cheat systems. They detect and respond to suspicious or unauthorized activities, maintaining a fair gaming environment.

Synchronization in Multiplayer Gaming

Synchronization is the heartbeat of multiplayer gaming, ensuring that every player experiences the same game world.

It involves several key aspects:

Player Position: In a multiplayer shooter, for example, the server synchronizes the positions of all players. When you see an opponent on your screen, the server ensures that your view matches theirs, preventing discrepancies or "teleporting" players.

Latency Compensation: Synchronization accounts for network latency, the delay in data transmission between your device and the server. Techniques like "lag compensation" ensure that your actions are registered fairly, even if there's a slight delay.

Interpolation: To smooth out movement and animations, the server uses interpolation. It predicts where objects or players will be between updates, creating a seamless experience.

Time Stamps: Every action in a multiplayer game is timestamped. This allows the server to order actions correctly and maintain a chronological sequence of events.

How It Works
Here's a simplified look at how server-side mechanics and synchronization function in a multiplayer game:

Player Action: You, as a player, perform an action, like shooting an enemy.

Data Transmission: Your game client sends this action data to the server.

Validation: The server receives your action, validates it, and calculates the outcome.

Synchronization: The server updates the game state and sends this information back to all connected clients.

Client Reconciliation: Your game client receives the updated game state from the server and reconciles it with your local prediction.

Smooth Gameplay: With synchronization in place, you and other players experience the same game world with minimal discrepancies.

Server-side mechanics and synchronization are the unsung heroes of multiplayer gaming, working behind the scenes to ensure that every action, every shot, and every victory is fair and consistent for players around the world. The next time you embark on a multiplayer gaming adventure, remember that these invisible forces are the ones making it all possible.

Chapter 6 - Real-time interactions and their challenges

In the vast expanse of multiplayer gaming, where players gather from across the globe for immersive adventures, there exists an intricate ballet behind the scenes. Player synchronization and authoritative servers are the unassuming choreographers orchestrating the seamless performance of online gaming. Let's unravel these foundational components and how they sculpt the captivating world of multiplayer gameplay.

The Essence of Player Synchronization

In the realm of multiplayer gaming, the magic lies in the synchronization of player actions across the digital landscape. It ensures that every movement, every shot fired, and every strategy executed is consistent and universally experienced:

Uniform Actions: Player synchronization guarantees that each action a player takes – be it running, jumping, or unleashing a powerful spell – unfolds consistently on all participants' screens.

Taming Latency: It tames the unruly beast known as latency, which causes delays in data transmission. Techniques like lag compensation help create a fluid and responsive gaming environment, where every action feels immediate.

Seamless Engagement: Synchronization involves techniques like interpolation and extrapolation, making sure that characters and objects move fluidly and harmoniously, resulting in a captivating gaming experience.

Chronological Precision: Timestamps are assigned to every action, meticulously preserving the chronological order of events, ensuring that the game's narrative unfolds seamlessly.

The Indispensable Role of Authoritative Servers

In the intricate tapestry of multiplayer gaming, authoritative servers serve as the lighthouses guiding the way:

Central Command: Multiplayer games pivot around the concept of a central authority – the authoritative server. This omnipotent entity oversees the entire game world, imposing rules and validating player actions.

Vigilant Validation: Player actions are meticulously scrutinized by the authoritative server, ensuring that they align with the game's rules and fairness guidelines.

Real-Time Stewardship: These servers are entrusted with the real-time management of the game's state. They monitor player positions, health statuses, scores, and an array of variables, harmonizing the experience across all connected clients.

Guardians of Fairness: Authoritative servers are steadfast guardians of fairness and security, implementing anti-cheat measures to protect the integrity of the gaming environment.

The Symphony of Operation

Here's a simplified rendition of how player synchronization and authoritative servers come together in multiplayer gaming:

Player Action: As a player, you execute an action within the game, like unleashing a mighty spell.

Transmission: Your action embarks on a digital journey to the authoritative server.

Validation: The server meticulously verifies your action, ensuring it adheres to the game's rules and spirit.

Synchronization: The server updates the game's state in real-time and shares this information with all connected clients.

Client Harmony: Your game client receives these updates and integrates them with your local predictions, creating a harmonious and synchronized experience.

Seamless Gameplay: With player synchronization and authoritative servers in command, you and fellow gamers traverse a virtual realm where every action feels natural and consistent.

Player synchronization and authoritative servers are the virtuoso architects shaping the immersive world of multiplayer gaming. They ensure that every tactical move, every tactical strike and every thrilling victory resonates uniformly for players across the globe. The next time you embark on a multiplayer gaming odyssey, pause to acknowledge these silent choreographers whose expertise makes it all possible.

Handling collisions, physics, and animations

Collisions within the gaming sphere signify the moment when the digital meets the real. It's the interaction between characters and objects that lends authenticity and engagement to the gaming experience:

Collision Detection: Behind the scenes, advanced algorithms continuously monitor the positions, shapes, and trajectories of objects, instantly detecting when these digital entities intersect.

Resolution Strategies: Once a collision is identified, the game engine must decide how to resolve it. Should a character bounce off a wall, shatter an obstacle, or simply slide away? These decisions make the virtual world feel dynamic and believable.

Immersive Feedback: The success of collision mechanics

lies in their ability to provide feedback. When a character impacts an object or another character, the resulting visual and auditory cues contribute to the player's sense of presence and realism.

Physics - Breathing Life into the Virtual Realm
Physics engines are the architects of virtual reality, using complex algorithms to simulate real-world physical principles. They introduce realism and consistency to the gaming experience:

Gravitational Pull: Physics engines meticulously apply gravity, allowing objects to fall, characters to jump, and puzzles to revolve around weight and balance.

Momentum and Inertia: Virtual objects adhere to the laws of momentum and inertia. This adds authenticity to vehicle handling, object manipulation, and the way characters move within the game world.

Friction and Impact: Surfaces exhibit friction, affecting how objects slide or roll, while impacts generate lifelike reactions like objects scattering upon an explosion.

Rag-doll Realism: To achieve lifelike character animations during combat or falls, some games employ rag-doll physics, permitting realistic reactions to forces.

Animations - The Heartbeat of Virtual Characters

Animations breathe vitality into gaming characters, endowing them with movements, emotions, and behaviours. They are the pulse of the virtual world:

Character Choreography: Characters are granted a rich repertoire of animations, encompassing everything from basic locomotion to intricate combat manoeuvrers. These animations blend seamlessly to produce fluid character actions.

Emotive Expressions: High-quality animations extend to facial expressions, conveying emotions and reactions that enhance players' emotional connections with the virtual personas they control.

Interaction with the Environment: Animations dictate how characters interact with objects in the game environment, whether it's opening a door, picking up an item, or navigating obstacles with realism.

Inverse Kinematics: This sophisticated technique ensures that character limbs and joints move organically, resulting in smooth and true-to-life interactions with the virtual surroundings.

The mastery of collisions, physics and animations forms the cornerstone of gaming's immersion. These intricate mechanics unite to create genuine interactions, supernatural feats, and lifelike characters, captivating players and transporting them to worlds of unfathomable wonder.

The next time you embark on a gaming voyage, take a moment to appreciate the artistry happening beneath the surface, breathing life into your digital adventures and redefining what's possible in the realm of virtual reality.

Chapter 7 - Turn-based and asynchronous multiplayer design

When it comes to multiplayer gaming, asynchronous gameplay mechanics is an innovative approach to multiplayer gaming which is reshaping our gaming experiences, offering new ways to interact, compete and explore virtual realms.

The Core of Asynchronous Gameplay Mechanics

At its heart, asynchronous gameplay mechanics enable players to participate in multiplayer experiences without the need for real-time, simultaneous interaction. Instead of engaging with opponents in a synchronized virtual space, players can take their turns independently, often at their own convenience. This shift from synchronous to asynchronous gameplay has opened up exciting possibilities across a wide spectrum of gaming genres.

How Asynchronous Gameplay Mechanics Function

Asynchronous gameplay mechanics enable players to take turns independently, often without time constraints. This approach includes turn-based dynamics, time-shifted competition, and notification systems to inform players when it's their turn or when opponents have made a move.

Turn-Based Dynamics: The most prevalent form of asynchronous gameplay is the turn-based model, where players take their turns sequentially, typically with no time constraints. This approach finds its home in strategy games, board games, and card games.

Time-Shifted Competition: Asynchronous multiplayer introduces a unique dimension where players can compete against recorded actions of others. For example, in racing games, you can race against a "ghost" of another player's best lap time.

Notification Systems: Many asynchronous games incorporate notification systems to inform players when it's their turn or when an opponent has made a move. This streamlined approach keeps the gaming experience flowing smoothly and allows players to engage at their own pace.

The Advantages of Asynchronous Gameplay Mechanics

Asynchronous gameplay mechanics offer flexible scheduling, allowing players to participate at their convenience, global competition by transcending time zones, and enhanced strategy with ample time for thoughtful decision-making, making them a versatile and inclusive approach to multiplayer gaming.

Flexible Scheduling: Asynchronous gameplay caters to the diverse schedules of players. You can make your moves or take your turns whenever it fits into your day, making it an ideal choice for gamers with busy lives.

Global Competition: Asynchronous multiplayer knows no borders. It enables players to compete with gaming enthusiasts from around the world, disregarding time zones and geographical limitations.

Enhanced Strategy: Turn-based asynchronous games often place a strong emphasis on strategy and critical thinking. Players have ample time to contemplate their moves, devise cunning tactics, and weigh their options carefully.

Prominent Examples
Words with Friends: This word puzzle game lets players engage in leisurely, turn-based wordplay with friends or random opponents, adding a social dimension to gaming.

Chess.com: An online chess platform that seamlessly combines real-time and asynchronous gameplay, allowing chess aficionados to enjoy the timeless game at their own pace.

Clash Royale: This mobile strategy game marries real-time and asynchronous elements, empowering players to construct decks and engage in epic battles with opponents.

Draw Something: A delightful drawing and guessing game where players take turns creating artful masterpieces and unravelling the drawings of others.

The Future of Asynchronous Gameplay
Asynchronous gameplay mechanics are on a continuous evolutionary journey, infiltrating various gaming genres and pushing boundaries. Game developers are at the forefront of exploring novel ways to incorporate asynchronous elements, granting players more avenues to engage with friends and competitors. Given the ever-expanding realm of mobile gaming and the call for flexibility in our gaming experiences, asynchronous gameplay is poised to play a pivotal role in shaping the future of gaming.

In summary, asynchronous gameplay mechanics mark a substantial transformation in the realm of multiplayer gaming. They offer gamers unparalleled flexibility, convenience, and a fresh perspective on competitive and strategic gameplay. Beyond mere turn-taking, asynchronous gaming redefines how we connect, compete, and revel in the virtual realms we cherish. It's not just a gaming revolution; it's an invitation to rediscover the joy of gaming on your terms.

Managing player actions across time zones

Managing player actions across different time zones in a multiplayer game is a complex task that game developers must carefully address during the design and development stages.

Here's how game developers deal with this challenge:

Turn-Based Systems: Turn-based multiplayer games are inherently suited for handling time zone differences. In these games, players take their turns one by one, often with no time pressure. This allows players from various time zones to play at their convenience. Developers ensure that the game server accurately records and maintains the order of turns, regardless of players' locations.

Asynchronous Gameplay: Asynchronous multiplayer games are designed explicitly to accommodate players in different time zones. In these games, players make their moves independently and receive notifications when it's their turn. Game developers implement robust notification systems to inform players when actions are required, ensuring that time zone disparities don't disrupt gameplay.

Server Timestamps: Game servers rely on precise timestamps to record player actions. These timestamps ensure that actions are processed in the correct chronological order, regardless of where players are located. This maintains the integrity of the game world's timeline and prevents any confusion caused by time zone differences.

Global Matchmaking: In games with matchmaking systems, developers often implement global matchmaking pools. This means that players from various time zones can be matched with one another. The matchmaking algorithm considers skill level and latency but doesn't restrict players based on their geographical location.

Scheduled Events: Some multiplayer games feature scheduled events or activities that occur at specific times. Developers must communicate these events clearly to players, taking into account time zone differences. This might involve displaying event times in the player's local time zone or using a universal time standard like Coordinated Universal Time (UTC).

Community Building: Developers encourage players to form communities and guilds within the game. These communities often include players from different time zones. Establishing clear communication channels and tools for community management helps players coordinate and plan activities across time zones.

Global Leader boards: In competitive multiplayer games, global leaderboards rank players based on their performance. These leaderboards typically display players from around the world, allowing for healthy competition regardless of time zone disparities.

Localization and Time Zone Support: Game developers often provide localization options, allowing players to choose their preferred language and, in some cases, their time zone. This personalization can enhance the player experience and make it easier for players to coordinate with others.

Ongoing Monitoring and Adjustments: Developers continuously monitor how players interact with the game across different time zones. They use player feedback and analytics to make adjustments, fine-tune gameplay, and address any issues related to time zone management.

Game developers employ a combination of design choices, notification systems, server technology, and community-building strategies to manage player actions across time zones in multiplayer games. The goal is to create an inclusive and enjoyable gaming experience that accommodates players from around the world, regardless of when they choose to play.

Creating engaging experiences in slow-paced games

Creating engaging experiences in slow-paced multiplayer games requires a delicate balance of game design elements and player engagement strategies. While fast-paced action games can captivate players with adrenaline-pumping sequences, slow-paced multiplayer games rely on different mechanics and techniques to keep players invested.

Here's how game developers craft engaging experiences in slow-paced multiplayer gaming:

Emphasis on Strategy: Slow-paced multiplayer games often revolve around strategy and decision-making. Game developers create intricate gameplay mechanics that challenge players to think critically and plan their moves ahead of time. This can include strategic positioning, resource management, and long-term planning.

Rich Storytelling: Incorporating a compelling narrative can immerse players in the game world and motivate them to keep playing. Slow-paced games have the advantage of allowing for deeper storytelling, with intricate plot-lines, character development, and world-building. This storytelling can be delivered through cutscenes, dialogues, and in-game lore.

Complex Progression Systems: To maintain player engagement, slow-paced games often feature complex progression systems. This can include skill trees, character customization, and unlockable content. These systems give players a sense of achievement and a reason to continue playing and improving.

Player Interaction: Multiplayer slow-paced games can encourage player interaction through cooperative or competitive gameplay. Collaborative experiences can foster teamwork and social connections, while competitive modes create a sense of rivalry and motivation to excel.

In-Game Events and Challenges: Developers frequently introduce in-game events, challenges, or objectives that keep players engaged. These events can provide opportunities for players to earn rewards, test their skills, and work toward long-term goals.

Regular Updates and Content: Keeping the game fresh with regular updates, patches, and additional content is crucial. This not only fixes any issues but also adds new challenges, features, and experiences to keep players interested.

Community Building: Encouraging the formation of a strong player community can enhance player engagement. Developers can create forums, social media platforms, or in-game chat systems where players can discuss strategies, share experiences, and connect with fellow gamers.

Balance Pacing: While slow-paced games are deliberate in their pacing, it's essential to balance moments of tranquillity with action or challenges. This prevents players from becoming too passive or bored during extended periods of inactivity.

Player Feedback: Developers should actively listen to player feedback and adapt the game accordingly. Player input can lead to improvements, bug fixes, and adjustments that enhance the overall experience.

Tutorials and Onboarding: Slow-paced games often have complex mechanics that require careful introduction. Well-designed tutorials and onboarding processes can help new players understand the game's intricacies and prevent frustration.

In essence, creating engaging experiences in slow-paced multiplayer games involves a combination of strategic depth, immersive storytelling, player interaction, and ongoing content updates. By carefully crafting these elements, game developers can ensure that players remain invested and find long-lasting enjoyment in their gaming experiences, even at a slower pace.

Cheating, Fair Play, and Security

In the immersive world of multiplayer gaming, a fair and

enjoyable experience is the cornerstone of the gaming community. To uphold this, game developers and platform providers have their hands full, addressing issues ranging from cheating to maintaining civility among players. In this article, we delve into the strategies used to combat cheating, promote fair play, and ensure security in multiplayer gaming, including punitive measures for disruptive behaviour.

The Battle Against Cheating

Cheating in multiplayer games is like trying to sneakily peek at your opponent's cards in a game of poker—it ruins the fun for everyone. Game developers employ several methods to detect and prevent cheating:

Anti-Cheat Software: Advanced anti-cheat software is integrated into many multiplayer games, actively scanning for cheats like aimbots, wallhacks, and other unfair advantages. When detected, cheaters are flagged or banned.

Player Reporting: Most games allow players to report suspected cheaters. These reports are reviewed by game moderators who investigate and take action if necessary.

Fair Play Initiatives: Developers often implement fair play initiatives, promoting the importance of honest competition. These campaigns encourage players to play by the rules and discourage cheating.

Regular Updates: Developers release regular game updates that not only fix bugs but also patch potential cheat methods. This ongoing cat-and-mouse game keeps cheaters on their toes.

Ensuring Fair Play

Fair play is the bedrock of multiplayer gaming, fostering an environment where players can compete on a level playing field. Strategies to ensure fairness include:

Matchmaking Algorithms: These algorithms aim to create

balanced matches, pitting players of similar skill levels against each other. This reduces the likelihood of one-sided, unfair matches.

Player Ratings: Many games use player ratings to match players with others of similar skill. This helps prevent experienced players from dominating newcomers.

Ranked Play: Ranked modes separate casual and competitive play. Players can choose the level of intensity they prefer, ensuring that everyone can enjoy the game at their own pace.

Reporting Systems: In addition to reporting cheating, players can report other disruptive behaviour, such as harassment, hate speech, or unsportsmanlike conduct.

Security Measures

Ensuring the security of player accounts and personal information is paramount. Game developers implement several security measures:

Two-Factor Authentication (2FA): 2FA adds an extra layer of security to player accounts, requiring an additional verification step beyond a password.

Data Encryption: Personal and financial information is encrypted to safeguard it from potential breaches.

Regular Audits: Security experts conduct routine audits to identify vulnerabilities and strengthen the game's security infrastructure.

Punishing Disruptive Behaviour

To maintain a positive and respectful gaming environment, platforms like Xbox Live have implemented punishment systems for disruptive behaviour:

Temporary and Permanent Bans: Players who engage in

cheating, harassment, hate speech, or other disruptive behaviours can face temporary or permanent bans. This serves as a deterrent and ensures that respectful players can enjoy the game without interference.

Communication Bans: Some platforms restrict players from using voice or text chat if they repeatedly engage in disruptive behaviour, promoting a more pleasant gaming experience for others.

Account Suspensions: In severe cases, accounts can be suspended or even permanently banned from a platform, depriving disruptive players of access to online gaming communities.

In the battle against cheating, the promotion of fair play, and the enhancement of security are ongoing efforts to maintain the integrity of multiplayer gaming. These initiatives ensure that players can enjoy the immersive worlds of multiplayer gaming in a secure and respectful environment.

Punitive measures serve as a strong reminder that, in the world of gaming, playing by the rules and showing respect to fellow players is not just a guideline but a prerequisite for a thriving gaming community.

Chapter 8 - Preventing and detecting cheating in multiplayer games

In the sprawling universe of multiplayer gaming, maintaining a level playing field is paramount to preserving the integrity of the experience. Game developers are at the forefront of this battle, deploying a formidable arsenal of methods to deter and detect cheating within their virtual realms. In this article, we delve into the strategies employed, both on the server and within the game's code, to prevent cheating and safeguard the sanctity of multiplayer gaming.

The Watchful Eye of Anti-Cheat Software

Client-Side Vigilance: Anti-cheat software acts as a guardian on the player's device, scanning game files and processes to uncover any unauthorized modifications or external cheat software that might tip the scales unfairly.

Server-Side Sentinel: Some anti-cheat measures are stationed directly on the game server. These sentinels monitor player actions and scrutinize the data sent to the server, sniffing out peculiar or suspicious behaviour.

Unmasking Anomalies Through Behaviour Analysis

Game developers employ sophisticated algorithms to scrutinize player behaviour, looking for patterns that deviate from the norm. This might entail detecting consistently pinpoint-accurate head shots or behaviours that defy statistical probability.

The Art of Anomaly Detection

Anomaly detection algorithms sift through a wealth of player data, hunting for statistical aberrations like unusually high kill-to-death ratios, unorthodox movement patterns, or gaping disparities in skill levels.

Player-Driven Vigilance

Developers often empower players by providing reporting systems. These allow gamers to flag suspected cheaters, prompting investigations conducted by either human moderators or automated algorithms.

Fostering Fair Play
Beyond the technological countermeasures, developers launch fair play initiatives that use in-game messaging, tutorials, and campaigns to instill the values of ethical gameplay and sportsmanship.

The Guardian of Server-Side Checks
On the server side, vigilant checks are instituted to authenticate the legitimacy of player actions. For instance, the server may validate the distance a player moves or the pace at which they execute actions.

Encrypted Vigilance in Data Transmission
To guard against tampering with network data packets, data transmitted between a player's client and the server is often encrypted, ensuring secure gameplay.

Regular Game Updates
Developers employ regular game updates not only to introduce new content but also to release security patches and modifications aimed at thwarting known cheating methods.

Harnessing Machine Learning and AI
Advanced anti-cheat systems leverage machine learning and artificial intelligence to identify and adapt to evolving cheating techniques. These systems analyze colossal datasets, unveiling patterns indicative of foul play.

The Stark Reality of Hardware Bans
As a last resort, developers may resort to hardware bans, effectively barring specific hardware components, such as GPUs or CPUs, from accessing the game—a stringent measure to deter cheaters.

Allies in the Cloud

Some game developers forge partnerships with third-party anti-cheat service providers who offer cloud-based solutions. These services possess the agility to detect and combat cheating in real-time, thanks to a network of interconnected detection methods.

In the ever-evolving battle against cheating in multiplayer gaming, developers remain vigilant, adapting their strategies and tools to keep the virtual battlegrounds fair and honourable. The effectiveness of these measures is a testament to the commitment of game developers to ensure that every player can revel in the joy of competition without the shadow of cheating darkening their experience.

Fairness in competitive gaming and esports

In the electrifying world of competitive gaming and esports, where pixelated heroes clash in virtual arenas, one word stands tall above all others: fairness. It's the linchpin that not only defines the essence of competitive gaming but also shapes its very future.

The Quest for Fairness

Fairness in competitive gaming and esports is about more than just rules and regulations; it's about ensuring that every player has an equal shot at victory. It begins with these core principles:

Equitable Rules and Regulations

In esports and competitive gaming, rules are the bedrock upon which every match is built. They must be transparent, unbiased, and consistently enforced. This includes rules about in-game behaviour, allowable equipment, and more.

Level Playing Field

Fairness demands that every player competes on a level playing field. This means no one should have an unfair advantage due to factors like superior hardware or network connectivity.

Balanced Gameplay

Game developers play a pivotal role in fostering fairness. Balancing characters, weapons, and maps ensures that no one strategy becomes dominant, promoting diverse and skill-based competition.

Anti-Cheat Measures

Cheating is the antithesis of fairness. Developers and tournament organizers employ stringent anti-cheat measures to detect and prevent cheating, leveling the competitive landscape.

Accessibility

To promote fairness, competitive gaming and esports should be accessible to all. This means ensuring that players from all backgrounds can participate, irrespective of socioeconomic factors.

The Role of Esports Organizations

Esports organizations play a critical role in upholding fairness. They are responsible for organizing and hosting tournaments, which means they must ensure that every competition adheres to strict fairness standards:

Player Contracts

Esports organizations establish contracts with players and teams, outlining the terms of competition and behaviour expectations. These contracts often include provisions regarding fair play and ethical conduct.

Governance and Oversight

Governing bodies like the Esports Integrity Commission (ESIC) exist to oversee competitive gaming and ensure fairness. They investigate allegations of cheating, match-fixing, and other breaches of fairness.

Player Support
Esports organizations provide support for players, including mental health resources, to ensure that the pressure of competition does not compromise fairness or well-being. Fairness Challenges in Esports

Despite the strides made in ensuring fairness, challenges persist. These include issues such as doping, match-fixing and disputes over player contracts. Esports organizations, game developers, and governing bodies must work together to address these challenges and maintain the integrity of the industry.

The Future of Fairness
As competitive gaming and esports continue to grow, the pursuit of fairness remains paramount. Esports will only thrive when every player can compete with confidence, knowing that victory is determined by skill, strategy, and dedication rather than unfair advantages.

In conclusion, fairness in competitive gaming and esports is not just an aspiration; it's a commitment. It's a pledge to uphold the spirit of competition, to create a level playing field, and to ensure that every player has the opportunity to reach for greatness. As the esports industry continues to evolve, it must do so with a steadfast commitment to fairness, for it is the beacon that guides the way forward into a more inclusive and equitable gaming future.

Communication and Social Dynamics

In the vast landscapes of multiplayer gaming, where gamers from every corner of the world converge, a dynamic and complex social ecosystem unfolds. Beyond the exhilarating gameplay and breathtaking graphics lies a world where communication and social interactions shape the gaming experience.

The Power of Connection

At its heart, multiplayer gaming is about connecting people. Players forge bonds, whether fleeting or enduring, with fellow gamers they may never meet in person. These connections are the lifeblood of the gaming community and contribute significantly to the overall experience.

Teamwork and Coordination
In team-based multiplayer games, communication is pivotal. Players must coordinate strategies, share information, and respond to rapidly changing situations. Effective teamwork often hinges on clear and concise communication.

Global Conversations
The gaming world is a global village where diverse cultures and languages intersect. Gamers routinely interact with individuals from different backgrounds, fostering cross-cultural exchanges and expanding horizons.

Friendships and Communities
Multiplayer games offer a platform for forming friendships and communities. Gamers connect through guilds, clans, and forums, finding like-minded individuals who share their passion.

The Dark Side - Toxicity and Misconduct
While multiplayer gaming has the power to unite, it can also expose players to a darker side of human interaction. Toxicity, harassment, and unsportsmanlike conduct are challenges that must be addressed:

Online Anonymity
The veil of online anonymity can embolden individuals to behave in ways they might never consider in real life. This anonymity can lead to harassment, hate speech, and disruptive behaviour.

Combatting Toxicity
Game developers have implemented systems to combat toxicity, including reporting mechanisms, chat filters, and

penalties for disruptive players. Esports organizations and gaming communities also take a stand against toxic behaviour.

Mental Health Awareness
The gaming industry is increasingly recognizing the importance of mental health. Online interactions can have a profound impact on players' mental well-being, prompting discussions and resources to support players' mental health.

A Platform for Expression

Multiplayer gaming is more than just gameplay; it's a canvas for self-expression. Players often customize their avatars, create unique in-game personas, and engage in creative activities within the game world.

Cosmetic Customization
Many multiplayer games offer extensive cosmetic customization options, allowing players to create unique characters, skins, and emotes that reflect their individuality.

Player-Created Content
Some games empower players to create content within the game, from custom maps and game modes to elaborate architectural feats in sandbox games.

Streaming and Content Creation
A growing number of players become content creators, streaming their gameplay and engaging with audiences. Platforms like Twitch and YouTube have turned gaming into a form of entertainment and self-expression.

Looking Ahead
As multiplayer gaming continues to evolve, so too will its communication and social dynamics. The future promises more immersive experiences, innovative ways to connect, and ongoing efforts to combat toxicity and promote inclusivity. In the end, multiplayer gaming is more than just pixels on a

screen; it's a vibrant, ever-changing world where players come together, forge connections and create memorable experiences.

Chapter 9 - In-game communication tools and systems

Within the captivating universe of multiplayer gaming, where alliances are forged and epic battles are waged, one integral element stands out—the power of communication. Beyond the dazzling graphics and intricate gameplay mechanics lies a realm of in-game communication tools and systems that give life to the social fabric of multiplayer gaming.

The Pulse of Multiplayer Interaction

In-game communication tools are the heartbeat of multiplayer gaming. They serve as the conduits through which players connect, collaborate, and celebrate victories. Let's explore the core components that fuel these interactive gaming experiences:

Voice Chat
Voice chat is the lifeline that allows players to converse using microphones or headsets. It's the medium through which strategies are devised, tactics are communicated and camaraderie is fostered.

Text Chat
Text chat is the written counterpart to voice communication, enabling players to type messages to each other within the game. It serves as a versatile tool for communication, especially in situations where voice chat may not be ideal.

Emotes and Pings
Emotes and pings provide players with a visual language to express emotions, share information, and highlight key objectives without the need for words. They are particularly useful in fast-paced gaming scenarios.

Party and Group Systems
Multiplayer games often feature party or group systems that

facilitate the formation of teams. These systems streamline communication and coordination among team members, enhancing the overall gaming experience.

The Inner Mechanisms of In-Game Communication

Beneath the surface, the seamless operation of in-game communication tools relies on intricate systems:

Voice Over IP (VoIP)
Voice chat systems utilize Voice over IP technology to transmit audio data between players. These systems manage voice quality, compression, and network optimization to ensure clear and lag-free communication.

Text Chat Servers
Text chat operates on dedicated servers responsible for transmitting text messages among players. These servers also include filters and moderation tools to maintain a respectful gaming environment.

Server Infrastructure
Game servers are the backbone of multiplayer gaming. They manage player connections, host game sessions, and oversee all in-game communication processes. Robust server setups ensure uninterrupted communication, even during peak gaming loads.

Encryption and Security
To safeguard player privacy and thwart eavesdropping, in-game communication is often encrypted. Security measures are in place to prevent unauthorized access and protect players from harassment.

The Social Tapestry

In-game communication tools transcend mere utility; they shape player interactions and weave intricate social connections:

Teamwork and Strategy

Effective communication is the linchpin of teamwork and strategic gameplay in multiplayer settings. It empowers players to coordinate actions, respond swiftly to challenges and adapt to evolving scenarios.

Friendships and Communities

Many profound friendships and gaming communities have sprouted from in-game interactions. Players bond, share experiences, and often create lasting connections that extend beyond the gaming world.

Esports and Competitive Play

In the competitive realm of esports, in-game communication stands as a pivotal element. Clear and precise communication can be the deciding factor between triumph and defeat.

As multiplayer gaming continues its evolution, so too will the landscape of in-game communication tools. Developers are exploring innovative avenues such as spatial audio, which replicates positional sound, and AI-driven chat moderation to elevate the gaming experience to new heights.

In closing, in-game communication tools are the unsung heroes of multiplayer gaming. They empower players to communicate, collaborate, and craft unforgettable experiences together. While they may seem like lines of code, these systems are the invisible threads that knit the rich tapestry of multiplayer gaming, transforming it into a vibrant universe where camaraderie, strategy and exploration reign supreme.

Toxic behaviour and fostering a positive community

In the vast, interconnected universe of online gaming, the atmosphere can vary from camaraderie and sportsmanship to a toxic battleground. The critical difference? The effort put into cultivating a positive gaming community. Achieving this involves a collective endeavour, with game developers, platform providers, and players all playing pivotal roles.

Crystal-Clear Code of Conduct
Establish and enforce a well-defined code of conduct that spells out acceptable behaviors and what's strictly off-limits. This includes a resolute stance against hate speech, harassment, and cheating.

Streamlined Reporting Systems
Design efficient reporting mechanisms that empower players to flag abusive or disruptive conduct. The commitment to swift review and appropriate action is vital.

Vigilant Moderation and Enforcement
Deploy dedicated moderators trained to monitor and enforce community guidelines. Their role is to address issues promptly, impartially, and efficiently to maintain a respectful atmosphere.

Education for All
Launch educational campaigns within games or on platforms to foster awareness about the importance of respectful communication and sportsmanship among players.

Positive Reinforcement
Reward commendable conduct and sportsmanship within the gaming environment. Recognizing and celebrating good behaviour incentivizes others to follow suit.

Unity Through Events
Organize community events, tournaments, and contests that promote cooperation and camaraderie. Such gatherings can help forge a profound sense of belonging.

Diversity and Inclusion
Ensure that games and gaming platforms reflect a diverse and inclusive spectrum of players. Representation matters in

fostering a welcoming and harmonious atmosphere.

Mentorship Initiatives
Develop mentorship programs where experienced players guide newcomers. This not only nurtures a sense of community but also eases the transition for new gamers.

Ears Open to Feedback
Actively seek feedback from the gaming community regarding their experiences and concerns. Implement this feedback to enhance policies and features continually.

Parental Control Empowerment
Develop robust parental control features that empower parents to protect younger players from inappropriate content and interactions. Educate parents about these controls.

Recognize Community Leaders
Acknowledge and incentivize community leaders who actively promote positive behavior and help maintain a friendly gaming atmosphere. Special titles or privileges can serve as incentives.

Guideline Workshops
Organize workshops or webinars that educate players about community guidelines and gaming etiquette. Encourage open discussions on topics like healthy competition and respect.

Transparency Matters
Maintain transparency in how rule violations are addressed and the ensuing consequences. This transparency helps players understand that inappropriate behavior carries repercussions.

Consequences, Consistently
Enforce consequences for rule violations consistently and equitably. Temporary suspensions or permanent bans may be necessary for severe infractions.

Lead by Example

Encourage game developers, platform providers, and influential players to set the standard with exemplary behaviour. Their actions set the tone for the entire gaming community.

Fostering a positive gaming community requires collective commitment. By putting these strategies into practice and nurturing a culture of respect, empathy, and inclusivity, we can collectively steer the gaming world away from toxicity and towards a realm of enjoyable, welcoming experiences for all players.

Inspiring teamwork, cooperation and player relationships

Multiplayer games have a unique ability to inspire teamwork, cooperation, and the formation of player relationships. These elements are often essential for success in many multiplayer titles and contribute significantly to the overall gaming experience. Here's how multiplayer games achieve this:

Shared Objectives

Multiplayer games often revolve around common goals and objectives that require players to collaborate. Whether it's capturing an enemy flag, completing a raid, or achieving victory in a team-based sport, these shared objectives encourage teamwork and cooperation.

Roles and Specializations

Many multiplayer games feature diverse character classes, roles, or specializations. Each player's unique abilities or skills contribute to the team's success, emphasizing the need for cooperation and strategy to make the most of everyone's strengths.

Communication

Effective communication is a cornerstone of multiplayer gaming. Players must share information, coordinate actions, and strategize in real-time. This often leads to the development of communication skills and fosters player relationships.

Team-Based Modes
Game modes designed specifically for teams encourage players to work together. These modes emphasize cooperation and reward teamwork, promoting positive player relationships.

Competitive Environment
In competitive multiplayer games, the desire to win can inspire players to cooperate closely with their teammates. The pursuit of victory often brings players together to strategize and execute coordinated moves.

In-Game Rewards
Multiplayer games often offer rewards or benefits for cooperative play. Whether it's shared loot, experience points, or in-game currency, these rewards incentivize players to collaborate and build relationships.

Team Building
Some multiplayer games incorporate team-building mechanics, where players are encouraged to form teams or guilds. These groups often become close-knit communities of players who share common goals and interests.

Player Roles and Responsibilities
In team-based games, players often assume specific roles and responsibilities. This division of labour encourages players to rely on one another and builds a sense of trust and dependency.

Challenges and Adversity
Facing formidable challenges or adversaries in multiplayer games can forge strong bonds among players. Overcoming difficult obstacles together creates a sense of achievement and camaraderie.

Friendly Competition

Even in competitive games, friendly competition can lead to the formation of player relationships. Competing against or alongside others fosters a sense of community and shared experiences.

Social Features

Many multiplayer games incorporate social features like friend lists, chat systems, and guilds or clans. These features make it easier for players to connect and build relationships within the game.

Esports and Tournaments

In the realm of esports and competitive gaming, teams and players often form close-knit units. Training, strategising, and competing together in tournaments strengthen player relationships.

Cross-Platform Play

Cross-platform multiplayer gaming allows players from different platforms to collaborate and compete. This expands the player pool and encourages diversity in player relationships.

In summary, multiplayer games inspire teamwork, cooperation, and player relationships through shared objectives, diverse roles, effective communication, and a competitive yet collaborative environment. These elements not only enhance the gaming experience but also contribute to the formation of lasting friendships and gaming communities.

Chapter 10 - Cross-platform play and its challenges

In the ever-evolving landscape of multiplayer gaming, one groundbreaking concept has captured the imagination of players worldwide: cross-platform play. This innovation promises to unite gamers regardless of their chosen platform, creating a more inclusive and expansive gaming ecosystem. However, this ambitious endeavor is not without its share of challenges.

The Vision of Cross-Platform Play

Cross-platform play, or "cross-play," seeks to break down the walls separating players on various gaming platforms. Whether you're gaming on a console, PC, or mobile device, the goal is to enable seamless interactions and gameplay between all players.

The potential benefits are substantial and are:

Expanded Player Pools
Cross-play opens the door to larger and more diverse player communities, reducing matchmaking times and enhancing the multiplayer experience.

Inclusivity
It allows friends and family to play together, regardless of their preferred gaming device, fostering a sense of inclusivity and connection.

Economic Accessibility
Players can enjoy games with friends without needing to invest in a specific platform, potentially reducing the financial barrier to entry.

Longevity
Cross-platform play can extend the life of multiplayer games

by ensuring a larger and more engaged player base.

The Hurdles on the Cross-play Journey

While cross-platform play holds immense promise, several challenges stand in the way of achieving this harmonious gaming utopia:

Technical Compatibility
Different gaming platforms have varying hardware capabilities, control schemes, and performance levels. Ensuring fair and balanced gameplay for all is a technical hurdle that developers must overcome.

Control Disparities
Players using keyboards and mice may have an advantage over those using controllers, affecting gameplay balance and fairness.

Player Skill Discrepancies
Integrating players of differing skill levels across platforms can lead to imbalanced matches and frustration.

Community Resistance
Some gaming communities may resist the integration of other platforms due to concerns about cheating, toxicity, or competitive fairness.

Platform Policies
Platform holders like Sony, Microsoft, and Nintendo have their own policies and requirements for cross-play, which can create logistical challenges for developers.

Game Development Costs
Implementing and maintaining cross-play features can be resource-intensive, particularly for smaller game studios.

Testing and Quality Assurance
Ensuring a bug-free and balanced cross-play experience

requires rigorous testing and quality assurance efforts.

The Path Forward

Despite these challenges, the momentum behind cross-platform play continues to grow. Many games now support cross-play in various forms, and developers are finding creative solutions to overcome technical and community-related hurdles.

Skill-Based Matchmaking
Developers can implement skill-based matchmaking to mitigate the impact of player skill discrepancies in cross-play matches.

Input-Based Matchmaking
Some games offer input-based matchmaking, pairing players with similar control methods (e.g., controller vs. controller, keyboard and mouse vs. keyboard and mouse).

Transparency and Fairness
Game developers can be transparent about cross-play mechanics and continually fine-tune them to ensure fairness.

Community Engagement
Fostering open communication with the player community can address concerns and build trust in the cross-play experience.

Continued Collaboration
Platform holders and game developers can collaborate closely to simplify the process of enabling cross-play and ensure a smooth user experience.

As multiplayer gaming continues to evolve, cross-platform play represents a significant step toward greater inclusivity and connectedness. While challenges persist, the determination to break down platform barriers fuels ongoing innovation, paving the way for a future where gamers from all walks of life can unite in the virtual realms they love.

Integration of multiplayer in single-player games

In the dynamic world of gaming, a remarkable shift is underway as single-player games embrace the spirit of cooperation and connection. These games, once known for their immersive solo narratives, are now weaving in multiplayer elements, reshaping the gaming landscape, and forging stronger bonds among players. This transformation responds to the growing desire for shared experiences and social interaction within the gaming community.

Picture stepping into a fantastical world, where a friend seamlessly joins your journey, enhancing your adventure without overshadowing it. Games like "Portal 2" and "A Way Out" make cooperative modes a reality, offering players the chance to collaborate in captivating environments. Meanwhile, titles like "Destiny 2" and "Sea of Thieves" invite players into persistent online realms, where they can embark on epic adventures together, sailing the high seas or exploring interstellar frontiers.

The integration of multiplayer elements is far from cosmetic; it's reshaping how we play and connect. Shared adventures, shared challenges, and shared triumphs are the cornerstones of this transformation, strengthening player relationships and creating lasting bonds. These gaming experiences often give rise to vibrant communities where players come together to strategize, celebrate achievements, and form meaningful connections.

However, this evolution isn't without its challenges. Achieving the delicate balance between single-player and multiplayer elements, maintaining a compelling narrative, and addressing technical hurdles like lag and server stability are some of the considerations developers must navigate.

Nonetheless, the journey continues, marked by innovation and boundless possibilities. Developers are experimenting with new ways to merge single-player narratives with multiplayer dynamics, igniting the industry's creative spirit. As we venture forward, we can enjoy the best of both worlds: epic solo adventures and collaborative quests with friends. Whether we choose to embark on these journeys solo or side by side, the adventure awaits in this ever-expanding gaming universe.

Innovations in augmented reality and virtual reality

In the thrilling world of multiplayer gaming, a fantastic frontier is emerging and it's all about the immersive wonders of augmented reality (AR) and virtual reality (VR). These game-changing technologies are breathing new life into multiplayer experiences, offering players a whole new level of engagement and connection.

Imagine stepping into a world where digital magic blends seamlessly with the real one. That's what AR does, enhancing social interactions by letting you play with virtual elements in your actual surroundings. "Pokemon GO" is a prime example, encouraging friends to team up and explore together, capturing virtual critters in the wild.

Now, think of VR as your ticket to entirely new realms. With VR headsets like Oculus Rift or HTC Vive, you're not just playing; you're living the game. Multiplayer VR gaming is all about sharing these incredible experiences with friends, no matter where they are. In games like "Beat Saber" or "Rec Room," you're not just talking tactics; you're physically dodging obstacles, waving lightsabers, and working together to conquer challenges.

These innovations aren't just about fancy visuals; they're about reimagining what multiplayer gaming means. With AR, your city streets become a gaming arena, and with VR, you're transported to otherworldly landscapes. Whether you're teaming up to take down virtual foes or working together to solve intricate puzzles, the possibilities are vast and endlessly exciting.

Beyond the gameplay, AR and VR also open up exciting new ways to socialize. Imagine meeting up with friends in virtual spaces, catching a concert together or tackling shared adventures. These technologies are redefining the boundaries of social gaming, bringing players closer even when they're continents apart.

Of course, there are hurdles like cost and technical requirements, but as technology evolves and becomes more accessible, the future of multiplayer gaming looks incredibly promising.

We're on the verge of a new era where gaming transcends the screen, offering immersive, interactive, and endlessly entertaining experiences that will redefine how we connect and play together.

Designing for Multiplayer Engagement

Crafting a multiplayer experience that keeps you engaged is a delightful puzzle that mixes gameplay mechanics, social vibes, and player joy. Let's dive into the secrets of making multiplayer games a blast!

At the heart of multiplayer magic lies the art of social interaction. A well-designed multiplayer game makes you feel connected, whether you're teaming up with buddies on a quest or battling it out for supremacy. It's all about those moments of camaraderie, the thrill of competition, and the shared excitement that can turn gaming into something truly special.

To pull this off, game designers have to whip up gameplay mechanics that encourage teamwork and rivalry. Think about cooperative multiplayer games; they're all about friends working together, each bringing their unique skills to the party. Competitive multiplayer games, on the other hand, are all about balance, where everyone gets a shot at glory. Finding the sweet spot between these elements is what makes a game engaging.

But wait, there's more! Game mechanics go beyond just playing nice with others. Features like character customization, levelling up, and earning rewards add layers of fun. Think about getting cool new stuff or climbing those leaderboards—keeps you coming back for more, right?

And hey, inclusivity and accessibility are super important. Games that welcome players of all skill levels create a diverse, friendly community. A warm and inclusive gaming gang is the secret sauce for keeping everyone engaged.

Now, here's a pro tip: game designers should be like avid listeners. Paying attention to player feedback, addressing concerns, and rolling out player-driven ideas can supercharge the game. It's like constantly adding spice to your favorite dish. Live-service models, with fresh updates and content, are a gamer's best friend for long-lasting enjoyment.

So there you have it, unlocking multiplayer magic through game design. It's not just about winning; it's about creating a world where you and your friends can laugh, strategize, and make awesome memories together. In this dynamic realm of multiplayer gaming, the key to happiness is keeping everyone engaged and having a blast!

Chapter 11 - Creating compelling objectives and rewards

One of the secrets to keeping players engaged and coming back for more in a game lies in the art of crafting compelling objectives and rewards. Let's dive into this dynamic duo and explore how they elevate multiplayer games to the next level.

The Quest for Compelling Objectives

Objectives in multiplayer games are like guiding stars, illuminating the path players should follow. Whether it's capturing a flag, securing a point, or completing a challenging raid, objectives provide purpose and structure to the gameplay.

Clear Goals
The first rule of crafting objectives is clarity. Players need to understand what they're striving for. Well-defined objectives ensure everyone is on the same page and fosters a sense of accomplishment when they're achieved.

Diversity is Key
Variety keeps the gaming experience fresh. Mixing up objectives - from team-based missions to individual challenges - prevents monotony and caters to different play-styles. This diversity keeps the game engaging over the long haul.

Storytelling Through Objectives
Many multiplayer games incorporate objectives into their narratives. Completing objectives advances the story, providing an immersive experience that makes players feel like heroes on a grand quest.

Balanced Challenge
The difficulty of objectives should be just right. They should be challenging enough to make players strive for improvement but not so hard that they become frustrating obstacles.

Rewards That Drive Progress

Rewards are the proverbial carrot on the stick, motivating players to push forward, improve their skills, and achieve greatness within the game.

Tangible Trophies

Rewards can come in various forms - from in-game currency to unique skins, powerful weapons, or rare items. These tangible rewards offer a tangible sense of accomplishment and progress.

Progression Systems

Many multiplayer games employ progression systems that reward players for their dedication and skill improvement. Levelling up, unlocking new abilities, or earning badges can be incredibly satisfying.

Exclusive Content

Unlocking exclusive content, such as character customizations or cosmetic items, adds prestige and personalization to the player's gaming experience.

Social Recognition

Leaderboards, trophies, and achievements can provide a sense of recognition and healthy competition among players. Bragging rights are a reward in themselves!

Fostering Engagement and Longevity

The art of designing compelling objectives and rewards is more than just a game mechanic; it's about creating an environment where players feel challenged, rewarded, and deeply immersed. It's a delicate dance that keeps players engaged, fuels their desire for progress, and cultivates a vibrant gaming community.

But the key to unlocking this magic isn't just in the design; it's in the constant dialogue between developers and players. Actively listening to player feedback, adjusting objectives and rewards, and rolling out fresh content are all part of the game.

In the end, creating compelling objectives and rewards isn't just about leveling up in a game; it's about levelling up the entire multiplayer gaming experience. It's about crafting worlds where players are heroes, where challenges are overcome, and where victories are sweetened by the rewards that come with them. So, game on, fellow players, and let the quest for compelling objectives and rewards drive your multiplayer adventures!

What are Micros-transactions used for in multiplayer gaming?

In the vibrant realm of multiplayer gaming, micro-transactions have become a pivotal element, allowing players to enhance their gaming experience and express their unique style. These small, in-game purchases, often conducted with real-world money or virtual currency, offer a range of benefits that can shape gameplay and player enjoyment. Let's dive into the world of micro-transactions and explore how they impact the multiplayer gaming landscape.

Cosmetic Creativity
One of the most common uses of micro-transactions is the acquisition of cosmetic items. Gamers can splurge on items like character skins, outfits, weapon camos, and emotes. While these items don't impact gameplay, they provide players with a canvas to showcase their individuality and creativity.

The Element of Surprise
Some multiplayer games introduce loot boxes or gacha systems, where players spend money to unlock randomized items. These can encompass cosmetic items but also in-game currency, boosts, or rare equipment. The allure of the unknown adds a layer of excitement, though it has sparked discussions about the potential for gambling-like mechanics.

Personalization Galore

Micro-transactions often grant players access to character customization options, including hairstyles, accessories, and appearance-altering items. This personalization enables players to craft avatars that reflect their identity and preferences.

A Boost to Performance
In specific multiplayer titles, micro-transactions offer boosts that enhance a player's in-game capabilities. These boosts can range from experience point (XP) bonuses to resource multipliers and power-ups, providing a competitive edge.

Expediting Progression
Progression accelerators are another micro-transaction category, designed to hasten the levelling-up process or expedite content unlocks. These options appeal to players seeking a faster-paced gaming journey.

Seasonal Delights
Many multiplayer games employ micro-transactions in the form of season passes or battle passes. These passes grant access to exclusive content, challenges, and rewards throughout a specific time frame, encouraging players to stay engaged and active.

Convenience at Hand
Convenience items, available through micro-transactions, aim to streamline gameplay. These can encompass inventory expansions, extra storage space, or quick-travel options, making the gaming experience smoother.

Currency Convenience
Players often have the option to purchase in-game currency using micro-transactions. This currency becomes a versatile resource, enabling the acquisition of various in-game items and services.

Expansion and DLC Goodies
While not always categorized as micro-transactions,

expansion packs and downloadable content (DLC) fall into a similar realm. These additional content offerings extend gameplay by introducing new storylines, maps, and gameplay elements.

Value-Packed Bundles
Micro-transactions may also manifest as starter packs or bundles. These combinations offer players a mix of items, currency, or exclusive content, presenting an attractive value proposition for those looking to kickstart their gaming adventure.

While micro-transactions undoubtedly enhance the gaming experience for many players, they also generate discussions about issues like pay-to-win mechanics, where monetary investments translate into significant in-game advantages.

Game developers grapple with the challenge of finding the right balance between micro-transactions that promote fair gameplay and generating revenue to sustain ongoing game development.

Why do people keep playing the same multiplayer game, day in and day out?

Ever wondered what makes multiplayer games so darn addictive? Well, it's not just the pixels on the screen; it's a mix of exciting factors that keep players coming back, day after day, to their favourite games.

Partying with Friends
Multiplayer games are the ultimate social hangout. You get to team up with friends, make new buddies, and share epic gaming moments. The friendships formed and the laughter shared can be a powerful magnet.

The Thrill of Competition
The heart-pounding thrill of competition is like no other. Gamers are driven to improve their skills and conquer

opponents, and that drive keeps them hitting the play button.

Feeling Accomplished

Achievements, badges, and levelling up – these are the bread and butter of multiplayer games. Completing goals and reaching milestones gives players an awesome sense of accomplishment.

Fresh Adventures Await

Developers often spice things up with new content – new maps, characters, weapons, you name it. These updates keep the gaming experience fresh and players eager to explore what's new.

Fear of Missing Out (FOMO)

You don't want to miss out on cool events, rewards, or limited-time goodies, right? FOMO is real in gaming, and it's a big reason why players log in regularly.

Where Everybody Knows Your Name

Being part of a gaming community feels like home. It's where you belong, share experiences, and connect with fellow gamers.

A Breather from Reality

Multiplayer games offer an escape from everyday stress. Immersive worlds and gameplay become a cosy cocoon where players unwind and forget their worries.

Your Alter Ego

In multiplayer games, your in-game achievements and avatar become a part of you. It's not just about winning; it's about self-expression.

Never-Ending Challenges

With multiplayer games, the challenge never stops. New opponents, strategies, and game modes constantly keep players on their toes.

The Developer Connection

Game developers who actively engage with players, listen to feedback, and make improvements create a bond with their audience. Feeling heard and valued keeps players engaged.

Friends' Influence

Friends have a big say in your gaming choices. If your pals are into a game, you're more likely to join in on the fun.

Seeing Progress

Multiplayer games with clear progression systems show players that they're getting better over time. That sense of growth is like a magnet pulling them back in.

Your Digital Kingdom

When you can customize your characters and collect virtual treasures, it feels like you're building your digital empire. That sense of ownership keeps players invested.

It's the unique combination of these elements that makes multiplayer gaming so addictively awesome. Whether you're chasing victories, forming friendships, or just having a blast, multiplayer games have a special place in our hearts and keep us coming back for more.

Chapter 12 - Technological trends and their impact

Let's talk tech and how it's turning multiplayer gaming into an epic adventure. The gaming world is buzzing with exciting innovations that are reshaping the way we play and connect with others in virtual realms. Here's a friendly peek into the latest tech trends that are levelling up multiplayer gaming.

Supercharged with 5G
Picture this: no more lag or connection hiccups. With the arrival of 5G networks, multiplayer gaming is set to become smoother and more responsive than ever before. Say goodbye to those frustrating lag spikes.

Cloud Gaming
Cloud gaming services like Google Stadia and NVIDIA GeForce NOW are making high-quality multiplayer gaming accessible to everyone. No need for super-powered devices; the cloud does the heavy lifting, letting you dive into multiplayer action hassle-free.

Dazzling Realism with Ray Tracing
Ready for jaw-dropping visuals? Ray tracing tech is turning multiplayer game worlds into visual masterpieces. Think lifelike lighting, stunning shadows, and reflections that'll leave you in awe.

VR and AR Adventures
Strap on your VR headset or step into the world of Augmented Reality (AR). These technologies are redefining multiplayer gaming, offering immersive experiences and real-time interactions that take gaming beyond the screen.

AI in Gaming
AI-controlled characters are getting smarter by the day. They're your challenging foes and dependable allies, making multiplayer gaming more exciting and unpredictable.

Cross-Platform Play

No matter if you're on a console, PC, or mobile, you can now team up and compete with friends across different platforms. It's like one big gaming family.

Game Streaming and Content Creation

Ever thought of becoming a gaming star? Platforms like Twitch and YouTube Gaming let you share your gaming adventures with the world in real time, and you can connect with fellow gamers from around the globe.

Blockchain and NFTs

The gaming world is embracing blockchain and Non-Fungible Tokens (NFTs). You can own, trade, and sell in-game items, making gaming not just a pastime but an economic venture too.

Feel the Game with Haptics and Audio

Get ready to feel the action! Haptic feedback controllers provide tactile sensations, while immersive audio tech lets you hear every detail, making your gaming experience more sensory-rich.

Get Creative with User-Made Content

Love crafting your own game worlds? Many multiplayer games now allow players to create and share custom content, from maps to game modes, opening up endless possibilities for fun.

These tech trends are more than just buzzwords; they're changing the way we game, connect, and explore virtual worlds. The future of multiplayer gaming is bright, and it's all thanks to these exciting tech marvels. So, grab your controllers, headsets, or keyboards and dive into the ever-evolving world of multiplayer gaming!

Ethical considerations in multiplayer game design

Within the expansive world of multiplayer gaming, ethical considerations have emerged as a pivotal aspect of game design. Developers grapple with multifaceted choices, ranging from monetization strategies that avoid creating an uneven playing field to fostering a positive and inclusive gaming environment that protects player well-being.

These ethical challenges require a delicate balance between profitability and fairness, transparency in micro-transactions, and the eradication of toxic behaviours, ensuring that multiplayer gaming remains a space where players of diverse backgrounds and ages can enjoy equitable and safe experiences.

Fair Play or Pay-to-Win?
It's a bit like a moral tightrope for game designers. They want to make games profitable but not at the cost of fairness. Nobody likes feeling that the game is rigged against them just because they haven't opened their wallets. Striking that balance is a real challenge.

Loot Boxes and Surprises
Imagine opening a treasure chest and finding... more treasure! That's the thrill of loot boxes, but sometimes it can feel like a gamble. Game designers have to be ethical about this, making sure players know what they're getting into and that it's all in good fun.

Balancing Fun and Responsibility
Games can be super immersive, but they shouldn't become a 24/7 job. Game designers need to think about how much is too much. They want us to have fun, but they also care about our well-being.

Spreading Positivity
In multiplayer, you meet all kinds of players. Some are super

cool, but others can be a real drag. Game designers have a duty to create spaces where everyone feels welcome and safe. No room for toxic behaviour!

Privacy and Keeping Secrets
Games gather a lot of info about us, but that doesn't mean it's open season for our personal data. Designers must be ethical custodians of our information, making sure it stays private and secure.

Everyone's Welcome
Games should be for everyone, regardless of who they are. Ethical designers work hard to include diverse characters and storylines, steering clear of stereotypes.

Being Sensitive Matters
Some games tackle heavy subjects. Designers need to handle them with care, making sure they don't hurt anyone's feelings or beliefs.

Shopping Should Be Fair
If you're buying something in a game, it should be clear, fair, and not sneaky. Ethical designers also make sure you can get help if things go wrong.

Protecting the Little Ones
We love playing games, but not all games are suitable for all ages. Designers need to keep an eye out for younger players, making sure they're safe and having age-appropriate fun.

Open Ears, Happy Gamers
Ethical game designers are like good listeners. They care about what players say, respond to feedback, and make changes to improve the gaming experience.

Thinking Green
Games have a part to play in saving the planet too. Designers can make choices to use less energy, helping to reduce the carbon footprint of gaming.

Ethical considerations in multiplayer game design are all about making gaming enjoyable, fair, and inclusive. It's like having good manners in the gaming world – everyone has more fun when we play by the rules and treat each other kindly. Game on, and let's keep multiplayer gaming a friendly and fantastic place to be!

Speculation on the next generation of multiplayer experiences

As technology propels us into the future at breakneck speed, the world of multiplayer gaming is poised for a transformation of epic proportions. The next generation of multiplayer experiences is shrouded in excitement, innovation, and limitless possibilities.

Let's embark on a speculative journey and explore what the future may hold for multiplayer gaming.

Hyper-Realistic Virtual Worlds
Imagine stepping into a multiplayer game that blurs the lines between the virtual and real worlds. Hyper-realistic graphics, driven by advancements like ray tracing and AI, will immerse players in environments that feel indistinguishable from reality. Every detail, from the rustling leaves to the falling raindrops, will contribute to an unparalleled sense of presence.

Seamless Cross-Platform Play
The boundaries that once separated gaming platforms will continue to blur. Cross-platform play will become the norm, allowing players on consoles, PCs, and mobile devices to unite in the same virtual realm. The days of debating which system to choose will be replaced with a universal gaming experience.

Infinite Player Freedom
Freedom will reign supreme in next-gen multiplayer gaming. Players will shape their experiences to an unprecedented

degree, with open-world games offering countless choices that ripple through the game's narrative. Every action will matter, creating personalized stories in shared online worlds.

AI-Powered Gameplay

Artificial intelligence will evolve from being just a part of the gaming experience to an integral aspect of multiplayer games. Advanced AI will create dynamic, ever-evolving worlds, enabling players to interact with intelligent NPCs that adapt to their actions, creating fresh challenges with each encounter.

Blockchain Integration

Blockchain technology and non-fungible tokens (NFTs) will find their place in multiplayer gaming. Players will truly own their in-game assets, and virtual economies will thrive. Rare and unique items will become a symbol of prestige, with a real-world value attached.

Full-Body Haptic Feedback

The era of immersive haptic feedback will arrive. Full-body suits equipped with tactile sensors will allow players to feel the heat of battle, the rush of wind, and the impact of every virtual step. These sensations will blur the line between the physical and virtual worlds.

Augmented Reality (AR) Integration

Augmented reality will step off our smartphones and into our multiplayer gaming experiences. AR glasses will overlay digital elements onto our real-world surroundings, creating augmented battlegrounds and shared adventures that unfold in our living rooms, parks, and cities.

Spectator-Centered Esports

Esports will reach new heights as next-gen multiplayer experiences cater to both players and spectators. Advanced streaming technologies will enable viewers to interact with the game and influence the narrative, turning esports into an engaging and collaborative spectator sport.

Quantum Computing and Instantaneous Gameplay
Quantum computing's power will unlock gameplay experiences we can barely fathom today. Complex simulations, real-time physics, and limitless creativity will be at our fingertips, delivering instantaneous and dynamic multiplayer interactions.

Limitless Exploration and Discovery
The allure of exploration will drive multiplayer gaming. Vast, uncharted virtual worlds will beckon adventurers, promising untold mysteries, treasures, and encounters with other players who share the same boundless curiosity.

The future of multiplayer gaming is a thrilling prospect, where boundaries blur, reality and fiction meld, and innovation knows no bounds.

As technology continues to advance, the only certainty is that the next generation of multiplayer experiences will redefine how we connect, play, and adventure together in the digital realms of tomorrow.

Other Books In The "Video Game" Series by this Author

Please check out some of my other titles on the topic of "Video Games" which is my favourite topic to write about:

- **"Level Up Your Gaming Career: A Comprehensive Guide To Become A Professional Gamer"** released in April 2023.

- **"The Art Of Video Games Testing: A Comprehensive Guide"** released in June 2023.

- **"Unveiling Game Design: From Concepts To Creations"** released in June 2023.

Find these titles on Amazon as an E-book or they can be ordered as a paperback edition where available.

Thank you.

Henry Hanley

www.ingramcontent.com/pod-product-compliance
Lightning Source LLC
La Vergne TN
LVHW041215050326
832903LV00021B/626